"The new edition of Sherman Billingsley's *Stork Club Cookbook and Bar Book* is a delicious treat and a vibrant, sparkling trip into the world of the most famous night club of the twentieth century. If one were to research the most glamorous club in the United States from 1930 thru the mid-1960s, there would be one club mentioned—The Stork Club! There was not a more sensational club in Manhattan, or anywhere else. 'Everything that rises must converge' and no doubt Flannery O'Conner meant at 'The Stork.' The food and ambience attracted youthful and beautiful debutantes like Brenda Frazer and Gloria Vanderbilt, and during World War II generals and uniformed soldiers laughed and danced with their wives and girlfriends. Movie star handsome John F. Kennedy brought many a date to the club, and the Roosevelts and the Duke and Duchess of Windsor frequented regularly. The most celebrated Broadway and Hollywood stars—Cary Grant, Gary Cooper, Marilyn Monroe and Joe DiMaggio, Lauren Bacall and Humphrey Bogart, Judy Garland, Bert Lahr, Ethel Merman, and giants like Ernest Hemingway and Orson Wells—all enjoyed evenings at The Stork. This was the place to be seen and the Cub Room was 'the room.' Sadly we cannot visit today, as it closed its doors in 1965, but we can taste the delicious cuisine of chef-in-chief, Gustave Reynaud as he directs us in its preparation, and enjoy an Omelette Gloria Vanderbilt or a Stuffed Squab Damon Runyon, followed by a Lucille Ball Pink Lady! This book contains over 100 recipes and a charming introduction by Shermane Billingsley, the club owner's daughter. The energy, the pulse of the brightest club that gleamed for over thirty years, can be experienced and tasted in this delightful, expanded edition."

— Jane Lahr, author, editor, agent

THE STORK
CLUB COOKBOOK
AND
BAR BOOK

WITH "THROW A STORK CLUB PARTY"

THE STORK
CLUB COOKBOOK
AND
BAR BOOK

Sherman Billingsley and Lucius Beebe

With Additional Material by

Shermane Billingsley and Ken Bloom

**EXCELSIOR
EDITIONS**

Excelsior Editions is an imprint of State University of New York Press

For information, contact State University of New York Press, Albany, NY

www.sunypress.edu

Library of Congress Cataloging-in-Publication Data
Names: Billingsley, Sherman, author | Lucius, Beebe, author
With Shermane Billingsley; introduction by Ken Bloom
Title: The Stork Club Cookbook and Bar Book / throw a Stork Club party
Description: Albany: State University of New York Press, introduction
and original material [2022]; The Stork Club Cookbook, Sherman
Billingsley [1952]; The Stork Club Bar Book, Rinehart & Company [1946].
"Throw Your Own Stork Club Party," Shermane Billingsley [2001] | Series:
Excelsior Editions | Includes bibliographical references and index.
Identifiers: ISBN 9781438490946 (paperback) | ISBN 9781438490953 (e-book)
Further information is available at the Library of Congress.

10 9 8 7 6 5 4 3 2 1

Contents

Introduction

Top on the list of New York nightclubs for thirty-five years, the Stork Club's legacy continues decades after its closing in 1965. The man behind the club was Sherman Billingsley, a one-time bootlegger who, a few years after serving a fifteen months' sentence in Leavenworth prison, left Oklahoma for the big city of New York where he joined fellow bootleggers in buying up drugstores as fronts for selling booze. Billingsley gave up the drugstore racket and decided to join forces with a mobster with whom he made acquaintance to establish a speakeasy designed for only the most worthy of clienteles—which basically meant if you were Black or Jewish you weren't welcome to enter the speakeasy (unless you were a Jewish performer of renown). It should be noted that Billingsley wasn't alone in his shunning of certain elements of society. In fact, only Barney Josephson's Café Society welcomed everyone.

Billingsley's partners and fellow felons soon lost interest in the club (no one knows who thought up the name the Stork Club), and Billingsley was left alone to turn the space into his idea of a clubhouse for the rich and famous.

It wasn't enough to just open a new speakeasy, but one had to find the customers. At first, the richest of the upper class wouldn't try a new club. So, Billingsley decided to open the club to the 500's children. He took out ads in the Yale and Harvard student newspapers. And to pay for the advertising, he gave chits to the staffs for free drinks at the new club. Soon, the younger generation was packing the club and enjoying the free booze. Word was passed up the family trees to the parents of the students and they began their occupation of the club. Most importantly, the parents paid for their drinks, and soon the Stork Club was fully adopted by the Smart Set as their preferred hangout.

Billingsley made sure that the club had something for everyone. So, each of the rooms and each of the floors had their own different experiences. When you first entered the club there was the bar, its own little island in the middle of the room. Then one could go through the cocktail lounge into the main dining room where you could dine, dance and table hop.

After the main dining room was the exclusive Cub Room, Billingsley's private hideout where he could play poker and hobnob with the most elite of guests. One of the habitués of the Cub Room was radio and newspaper personality Walter Winchell who commandeered Table 50 and from which he broadcast his radio show, thereby giving priceless publicity for the club. And Winchell also got his haircuts there. Some wag said that Winchell was "a man without a private life at all, who was always onstage." And Sherman cosseted Winchell because the reporter was instrumental in putting the Stork Club on the map and keeping it there. What gossip wasn't covered by Winchell was offered by Billingsley to other denizens of the fourth estate.

If you continued upstairs from the Cub Room, you'd find the Loners' Room, designed for unaccompanied guests to eat alone in privacy. And finally, there was the Blessed Event Room (as Winchell dubbed it), which held private parties.

Much of Billingsley's time was fending off gangsters who wanted in, the government of New York, the Feds who wanted to shut him down during Prohibition, and his own employees who wanted to unionize. It was almost a game—a game he sometimes won and sometimes lost.

As you can see from Shermane Billingsley's accompanying memoir of the club, life there was always an adventure. Despite the maelstrom surrounding the club, for the guests it was a welcome oasis from the outside world. The clubhouse atmosphere extended beyond the Cub Room. The dining room hosted well-dressed and well-to-do patrons with an occasional someone dropping by from the states between New York and California.

Billingsley's largess had a lot to do with the stars' adopting the club as a home base when in New York. Expensive jewelry was bestowed on favored women. Cases of champagne were sent to regular denizens of the club. The Duke and Duchess of Windsor were given two cases of fine champagne. Some received bottles of the club's own perfume, Sortilege. Other gift bottles contained various alcoholic beverages of the highest quality (which were illegal for a time). Al Jolson was gifted a vicuna coat; President Eisenhower and First Lady Mamie, Errol Flynn, Cary Grant, Mayor Wagner, and many others received gifts that assured their continued loyalty.

The name Stork Club was recognized throughout the world, a symbol of smart sophistication. And practically every entertainment medium celebrated the club. Winchell had a lock on the radio audience with his broadcasts from the club. Starting in 1950, CBS Television broadcast the series *The Stork Club*, which lasted until 1955. And the club was used as a symbol of the smart set in many movies, most notably in 1945's aptly titled *The Stork Club*. Alfred Hitchcock's film *The Wrong Man* was shot on location in the club, and many others featured the club as a shorthand for high society.

Unlike many bars the club had an extensive menu. Many of the dishes on the carte du jour are memories today, such as Consommé Julienne, Jelly Madrilène, Vichyssoise, Jumbo Poached Frog's Legs, Boneless Stuffed Cornish Hen a la Walter Winchell, Cherries Jubilee, Coupe Nesselrode, and many others. There was even an entire section of the menu devoted to Chinese food with Chop Suey, Hung Yar Gai Ding (Almond Chicken), Pon Care Lot Jill Gai (Sliced Chicken with Tomato and Green Peppers), and more.

Today, watering holes such as the Stork Club are but a distant memory. The name and reputation go on over a half-century since it closed its doors for good. But some things do remain, such as this reprinting of the Stork Club's bar recipes.

Restaurants and clubs today don't feature exotic mixed drinks. Beer, wine, and fancy cocktails with intriguing ingredients seem to be a thing of the past.

Looking back, those heady days at the Stork Club were a respite from the outside world where crime, wars, and an overall diminishment of culture and class existed outside the walls. Today, life can be difficult in new and different ways. Perhaps just reading this book can offer a respite from the outside world. But think about trying one of these recipes while you sip your drink.

At Home at the Stork Club

Shermane Billingsley as told to Ken Bloom

As a child, I lived in a number of apartments, a townhouse, and our farm in Pound Ridge, but the place that I called home was the Stork Club. It was where I went after school, to have a Coca-Cola, do my homework, and sit with my dad. It was where we celebrated Thanksgiving, Christmas, and Easter, at our family table. No matter what the occasion, that's where we were. It was really home to me.

When I was seven or eight, it started to dawn on me that other people didn't have the same experiences as I did. I guess it was when my father and I would be walking down the street and people greeted him. And there was a certain deference toward him amongst the people that worked for him. I guess that's when I started to think, "Hmmm. He's a little bit of a different dad than my friends' fathers."

My friends were the children of members of the club. Bert Lahr's daughter Janie, Gary Cooper's daughter Maria, Jack Benny's daughter Joan. We all knew each other and still to this day we're in touch. However, it wasn't just the children of celebrities that I got to know. As a little girl my thrill was meeting William Boyd, Hopalong Cassidy. He was one of the nicest human beings I ever met. And later on there was Jack Webb from Dragnet. Yul Brynner was working on the Stork Club television show. I knew Yul very well. But one day after not seeing him for a year or so, he came into the club wearing his costume for The King and I. I only saw this very bizarre person who scared the dickens out of me and I screamed. And he burst out laughing and I immediately knew who he was.

I remember that Dolores Grey sent tickets to the musical Destry Rides Again for a couple of friends and myself. She invited us to come backstage after the show. We were escorted to her dressing room. It was lovely. There was a knock, knock, knock on the door. She went to answer it and in comes Cary Grant. We were a bunch of fourteen-year-olds and we thought we were going to die!

When I went away to college it was the first time I had lived anywhere but the Upper East Side. I loved college and meeting people from diverse backgrounds and that's when I truly realized my life wasn't typical.

My father had no intentions of going into the speakeasy business. He was a licensed real estate broker. In 1929, a couple of fellas from Oklahoma, so the story goes, were looking for a place to open a speakeasy and they asked my father if he could find them a suitable place. The men thought it was great and told my father they wanted him to come in as a partner. At that time, he didn't know anything about the restaurant business, but even so they assured him that he would be a full partner and they would run the place. Lo and behold, less than a year later, they told him they were homesick and wanted to go back to Oklahoma. They gave him their keys and said, "Here it is, you run it." And they walked away giving him the entire business.

His first thought was, "Oh my god, what do I do?" He had to learn while on the job. The first weeks weren't going so well. He used to tell a story how he'd stand at the front door with his major domo, Gregory Pavlides. They'd stand there and play a game: How many cars will pass by before one stops at the club? And many nights no cars stopped. He was thinking that maybe he'd have to give up the business when the writer Heywood Hale Broun accidentally walked into the place thinking it was a funeral parlor. Instead of finding corpses, Broun found a lot of booze. He quickly spread the word among his friends, including the famed singer of bawdy songs, Texas Guinan. She, in turn, tipped off newspaper columnist and radio personality, Walter Winchell, whose influence spread throughout the country. Winchell broadcast his radio show from the club's exclusive Cub Room. He would often feature the club in his Hearst newspaper column and on his radio show. And little by little, word got out and people started coming. Soon the tiny speakeasy couldn't handle all the regular customers and the throngs who came to ogle the regulars. The club moved two or three times before my father found its final location at 3 East 53rd Street where Paley Park is now.

My father would have made a very good drill sergeant. He ran a very tight group. There was a chain of command and he, of course, was at the head. And people were expected to follow orders and not to question them. He could also be very generous. He got to know the staff's families. Greg Pavlides started out as an attendant in the men's room; he ended up being known as "Sherman's shadow." Only Greg could interpret my father's hand signals, which could mean "send a round of drinks" or "get this guy outta here." In fact, a lot of the staff were with him for 20 or 30 or more years. At my father's funeral, I was happy to see the number of staff that attended. People loyal to him through thick and thin, even through the problems with the unions.

My father was always having a bit of a problem with the Mafia wanting to infiltrate the business. So, naturally, there was a lot of rivalry and threats to the family. In the building that housed the club, he had an apartment. If shady characters were waiting outside the club, he took the fire escape down from the apartment to the nightclub without having to walk into the street.

At one point he was worried about my sister, Jacqueline, being kidnapped by bad guys keeping an eye on the family. So, my mother's aunt picked her up, and my dad followed their car over the George Washington Bridge. Around the center of the span his car mysteriously happened to have a breakdown, blocking the traffic behind him. He stopped the car and waited till my aunt and Jacqueline were well on their way. Those were the little adventures I heard about when I was growing up.

Around the late '40s, the first time the staff went on strike, other union members supported them. We couldn't get the laundry or groceries delivered or the garbage picked up, and my father had to hire all private contractors. What was fascinating to me is that he was only one man: One man against all of the unions. That to me was quite amazing.

Even though his staff was picketing, he understood their reasons and in a way sympathized with them. Once he was watching the staff marching with their signs in the bitter, bitter cold. He sent out glasses of brandy to warm them up.

Of course, strikes still had to be taken seriously. But they also brought out his playfulness. I can remember when some of the staff was picketing the restaurant, my father went up on the roof of 3 East 53rd Street and dropped water bombs on the picketers! Another time and another union picket line was marching in front of the club. At my father's urging, some of the Eileen Ford models who were habitués of the club marched opposite the staff's picket line. The models carried signs reading: "We love the Stork"; "The Stork is cute"; "We love Sherm." And so we had two groups of pickets marching at the same time. It was quite a contrast and lightened the stress for everyone.

As he was with the unions so he was with the family. He could be tough when necessary and also fun and playful. He was a strict dad. He set the rules dictating what my two sisters and I were and were not allowed to do, but he was always an available d and a very nurturing dad. So we saw different sides of him.

My mother was very much in the shadows in many, many ways. She was quite a beautiful lady and my father was quite a jealous man. She was a typical mom and housewife; in charge of us doing our homework and her attending school functions. She wasn't someone who liked to draw attention or be in the limelight.

She left all of that to my father. My mother never went to the Club in the evening. Customers would have too much to drink, didn't realize that she was the boss's wife, and become personal. So, she and her friends would go at lunch when the patrons were mainly businessmen, regulars who worked in the neighborhood, and the cosmetic and fashion people from Elizabeth Arden and Ford models. Some of the models were a little self-conscious that they were recognized but they also got a kick out of being seen. And the ladies who lunched enjoyed seeing what the models were wearing and how they were doing their hair.

These were the faces that I learned to recognize. As my father used to say, the best décor you could possibly have are the people. And by "people" he was referring mostly to the beautiful women. So, between the models and the starlets, it was a very attractive group of people.

During the war, we had Army generals at the club, including none other than General MacArthur. They would commandeer a table and sit in whispered discussions while drawing diagrams on tablecloths: drawings of Western Europe and troop movements. And I can remember my father was saying, "Oh my god. We can't send these tablecloths to the Chinese laundry." So the cloths were destroyed. I recall seeing Hedy Lamarr sitting with the Generals and members of the War Department. She was working with composer George Antheil on a radio signaling device that would make it impossible for the enemies to decode the Allies' messages. It became the precursor of radar.

Eventually the Cub Room was created exclusively for the celebrities, a place where they could let their hair down and relax and be out of the eye of the public ogling and asking for autographs and paparazzi snapping photos in their faces.

When the Stork Club television show was running, things changed a bit. The club became a sort of tourist attraction. You always had your fingers crossed that someone like Cary Grant would be there so the tourists could go back home and brag, "Yes! We saw the Stork Club!" So, we had our regular year-round trade and the tourist trade and the celebrity group.

The end was difficult because my father was a fighter. And my mother begged him, "Sherman. Fold the place. Please!" Governors from Texas and Nevada asked him to move the club out west where he wouldn't have these problems with the unions. Jack Dempsey's Restaurant and The Sign of the Dove were also having union problems and they closed. My father was the last one standing. Basically, at the end he lost almost all his money and he lost his health. It was a pyrrhic victory.

He had a good life. A very exciting life and the satisfaction of having been successful. It was the life that he wanted. Too many people have the life they don't want and feel stuck. He did it his way. You couldn't take him away from the Stork Club. It was open 365 days a year so he was there 365 days a year. To get him to take a vacation was ridiculous. We used to go to a place named the Lake Placid Club. He would be there for two nights and at ten o'clock at night he'd say, "Where is everybody? Where'd everybody go?" He just wasn't used to that. He loved the club. That was his home and his passion.

The Stork Club is my dad's legacy but I think it also is an example of the historical significance of the era. The other clubs didn't have the mystique that the Stork Club had. Every day was an adventure. It was the celebrities, the generals, Broadway and Hollywood stars, the high life, and the lowbrows. It was the crossroads of the world in its little microcosm. And I was there looking and learning and growing up. I wouldn't have changed a thing.

About Sherman Billingsley, the Stork Club, and *The Stork Club Cookbook* and *The Stork Club Bar Book*

Ken Bloom

Top on the list of New York nightclubs for thirty-five years, The Stork Club's legacy continues decades after its closing in 1965. The man behind the club was Sherman Billingsley, a one-time bootlegger who, a few years after serving fifteen months sentence in Leavenworth prison, left Oklahoma for the big city of New York where he joined fellow bootleggers in buying up drugstores as fronts for selling booze. Billingsley gave up the drugstore racket when he was approached by two acquaintances from Oklahoma who asked for his help to establish a speakeasy designed for only the worthiest clienteles. Which basically meant if you were Black or Jewish you weren't welcome to enter the speakeasy (unless you were a Jewish performer of renown). It should be noted that Billingsley wasn't alone in his shunning of certain elements of society. In fact, only Barney Josephson's Café Society welcomed everyone.

Soon after opening Billingsley's original partners disappeared (no one knows who thought up the name the Stork Club) and were replaced by notorious mobsters Owney Madden, Big Bill Dwyer, and Frenchy De Mange. They allowed Billingsley to run the new enterprise, and he turned it into his idea of a clubhouse for the rich and famous.

It wasn't enough to just open a new speakeasy but one had to find the customers. At first, the richest of the upper class wouldn't try a new club. So, Billingsley decided to open the club to the 500's children. He took out ads in the Yale and Harvard student newspapers. And to pay for the advertising, he gave chits to the staffs for free drinks at the new club. Soon, the younger generation was packing the club and enjoying the free booze. Word was passed up the family trees to the parents of the students and they began their occupation of the club. Most importantly, the parents paid for their drinks and soon the Stork Club was fully adopted by the Smart Set as their preferred hangout.

Billingsley made sure that the club had something for everyone. So, each of the rooms and each of the floors had their own different experiences. When you first entered the club there was the bar, its own little island in the middle of the room. Then one could go through the cocktail lounge into the main dining room where you could dine, dance, and table hop.

After the main dining room was the exclusive Cub Room, Billingsley's private hideout where he could play poker and hobnob with the most elite of guests. One of the habitués of the Cub Room was radio and newspaper personality, Walter Winchell, who commandeered Table 50 and from which he broadcast his radio show, thereby giving priceless publicity for the club–and Winchell also got his haircuts there. Some wag said that Winchell was, "A man without a private life at all, who was always onstage." Sherman cosseted Winchell because the reporter was instrumental in putting the Stork Club on the map and keeping it there. What gossip wasn't covered by Winchell was offered by Billingsley to other denizens of the fourth estate.

If you continued upstairs from the Cub Room, you'd find the Loners' Room, designed for unaccompanied guests to eat alone in privacy. And finally, there was the Blessed Event Room (as Winchell dubbed it) which held private parties.

Much of Billingsley's time was spent fending off gangsters who wanted in, the government of New York City, the Feds who wanted to shut him down during Prohibition, and his own employees who wanted to unionize. It was almost a game—a game he sometime won and sometimes lost.

As you can see from Shermane Billingsley's accompanying memoir of the club, life there was always an adventure. Despite the maelstrom surrounding the club, for the guests it was a welcome oasis from the outside world. The club-house atmosphere extended beyond the Cub Room. The dining room hosted well-dressed and well-to-do patrons with an occasional someone dropping by from the states between New York and California.

Billingsley's largess had a lot to do with the stars' adopting the club as a home base when in New York. Expensive jewelry was bestowed on favored women. Cases of champagne were sent to regular denizen's of the club, including the Duke and Duchess of Windsor, who were given two cases. Some received bottles of the club's own perfume, Sortilege. Other gift bottles contained various alcoholic beverages of the highest quality (which were illegal for a time). Al Jolson was gifted a vicuna coat, and President Eisenhower and First Lady Mamie, Errol Flynn, Cary Grant, Mayor Wagner, and many others received gifts that assured their continued loyalty.

The name Stork Club was recognized throughout the world, a symbol of smart sophistication. And practically every entertainment medium celebrated the club. Winchell had a lock on the radio audience with his broadcasts from the club. Starting in 1950, CBS Television broadcast the series, *The Stork Club*, which lasted until 1955. And the club was used as a symbol of the smart set in many movies, most notably in 1945's aptly titled, *The Stork Club*. Alfred Hitchcock's film, *The Wrong Man* was shot on location in the club and many others featured the club as a shorthand for high society.

Unlike many bars, the club had an extensive menu. Many of the dishes on the carte du jour are memories today, including Consomme Julienne, Jelly Madelene, Vichyssoise, Jumbo Poached Frog's Legs, Boneless Stuffed Cornish Hen a la Walter Winchell, Cherries Jubilee, Coupe Nesselrode, and many others. There was even an entire section of the menu devoted to Chinese food—then a somewhat exotic novelty–with Chop Suey, Hung Yar Gai Ding (Almond Chicken), Pon Care Lot Jill Gai (Sliced Chicken with Tomato and Green Peppers), and more. During the '50s, Sherman self-published *The Stork Club Cookbook* to allow people who couldn't visit the club to recreate the experience at home. To add to the fun, Shermane had prepared her own essay, "How to Give A Stork Club Party," for an A-to-Z guide to the entire experience.

Today, watering holes such as the Stork Club are but a distant memory. But some things do remain. For example, this reprinting of the Stork Club's bar recipes. There has been an upswing in interest in the exotic mixed cocktails that were part and parcel of the Prohibition era. Society columnist and colorful figure Lucius Beebe compiled *The Stork Club Bar Book* in 1946 and it remains a classic reference work for mixologists today.

Looking back, those heady days at the Stork Club were a respite from the outside world where crime, wars, and an overall diminishment of culture and class existed outside the walls. Today, life can be difficult in new and different ways. Perhaps just reading this book can offer a respite from the outside world. But think about trying one of these recipes while you sip your drink.

The Stork Club Cookbook

Sherman Billingsley

ONE HUNDRED FAMOUS
STORK CLUB RECIPES

MAY · COSMOPOLITAN · 1947

Mr. "B"
and
his

STORK CLUB

The only night-club owner listed in Who's Who in America is Sherman Billingsley. The fine type following his last and first name in the July supplement to the 1943 edition of that collection of big-shot biographies begins with ". . . owner, Stork Club. Born in Enid, Oklahoma, March 10, 1900. Educated in grade schools in Oklahoma . . ."

Now I have nothing against Who's Who in America, but that seems to be a mighty dull way to make a reader acquainted with the proprietor and host of a colorful and glamorous institution on Fifty-third Street, Manhattan, U.S.A., which future historians may refer to as the Mermaid Tavern of our time. A Mermaid

The last magazine article of one of America's favorite reporters. It's about a very famous tavern and its equally famous landlord

By Damon Runyon

At my personal request, our Chef-in-Chief, Gustave Reynaud, has consented to make available to you these directions for some of the Stork Club's most titillating dishes. Monsieur Reynaud commands seventeen cooks in preparing them, but when I asked him if he was sure Mrs. Average Housewife would be able to manage them, he flicked his finger and murmured, *Mais oui*.

It's fun to be fancy. Particularly when you can be fancy without being fussy. It's not an easy combination to achieve, but we think you will find the following recipes easy to make and fun to serve. I am assured you'll be able to "throw them together" quite as easily as he does. Let me know how your finished products compare with Reynaud's.

And what is good food without good drink? The Stork's head barman, Nathaniel Cook has opened his secret archives to reveal formulas for the Club's most popular drinks. Offered herein are Cookie's contributions to the practical humanities.

S.B.

POTAGES

ONION SOUP AU GRATIN

2 cups sliced onions
2 tablespoons vegetable oil
1 tablespoon butter
5 cups brown soup stock (any kind)
1 tablespoon cornstarch
6 thick slices toasted French bread
3/4 cup grated cheese

Cook onions in oil and butter until soft and caramelized. Add cornstarch, stirring well, stock, salt, and pepper. Bring to a boil, place square of toast in each individual soup dish, ladle out the boiling soup and sprinkle thickly with grated cheese. Serves six.

CONSOMMÉ JULIENNE

4 cups consomme
1 tablespoon julienne carrots
1 tablespoon julienne turnips
1 tablespoon julienne leeks

Cook the vegetables for the garnish separately in boiling salted water until just tender. Drain and rinse them; then put them into a warmed tureen. Meanwhile, heat the consommé to boiling point. Pour the hot consommé over the vegetables, and serve. Serves four.

TURTLE SOUP

3 tablespoons olive oil
1 cup sifted all-purpose flour
1 cup finely-chopped green onions
1/2 cup finely-cut fresh parsley
2 quarts chicken stock
1 cup tomato sauce
4 large hard boiled eggs, finely chopped
1/2 cup finely-chopped lemon with the peel
1/2 teaspoon cayenne pepper
salt and pepper, to taste
2 1/2 pounds clean turtle meat, cut into 1/2 inch pieces.

Heat olive oil in a large pot over medium flame, then add the flour, stirring constantly until you have a dark roux. Add the green onions and parsley and cook, stirring until the onions are clear. Stir in the stock, tomato sauce, and lemon, and eggs; season with the salt and cayenne pepper. Lower the temperature to a simmer while you brown the turtle meat. Add the turtle meat to the stock; cover and simmer 2 hours. Serves six.

FRESH VEGETABLE SOUP

2 quarts chicken stock
3 tablespoons chicken base
1/4 teaspoon pepper
1/8 teaspoon salt
2 bay leaves
8 cloves garlic, crushed
2 stalks celery, thinly sliced
1/2 Bermuda onion, thinly sliced
1 large red pepper, chopped
12 baby carrots, thinly sliced
5 mushrooms, thinly sliced
1 scallion, sliced in one-inch pieces

Put everything into a soup pot and simmer gently for 1 to 2 hours, adding water as needed. Serves six.

CREAM OF CHICKEN SOUP

2 tablespoons butter
1/4 cup flour
3 cup chicken broth
1/2 cup chopped celery

1/4 cup chopped onion
1 cup cream
3 chicken breasts
salt and pepper, to taste

Boil chicken, celery and onion until done. Remove chicken and shread meat; reserve broth. Melt butter in top of double boiler over direct heat. Slowly stir in flour. Stir in broth and cream. Cook until smooth and thick. Add shredded chicken. Add salt and pepper to taste. Serves six.

CREAM OF TOMATO SOUP

1 stick butter
2 cups sliced onions
3 (14-ounce) cans whole stewed tomatoes, chopped
2 cups cream
salt and pepper, to taste

Cook onions in butter until golden brown. Add tomatoes with juice and cook for 30 minutes. Pass mixture through a sieve. Scald cream in another saucepan and stir it into tomato mixture. Heat through (do not boil). Season with salt and pepper. Serves six.

JELLY MADRILÈNE

2 (12 1/2-ounce) cans madrilene
1/2 cup Madeira
1/2 cup heavy cream
1/2 teaspoon salt

Warm madrilene just until soup liquefies. Remove from heat, stir in Madeira and chill at least 4 hours, or overnight. Break up jellied madrilene with a fork and serve in soup bowls. Just before serving, beat heavy cream and salt until cream is stiff. Top each serving with some of the salted whipped cream. Serves six.

VICHYSSOISE (COLD)

4 cups sliced leeks, white part
4 cups diced potatoes
6 cups water
1 1/2 to 2 teaspoons salt or to taste
1/2 cup heavy cream

1 tablespoon parsley, minced
salt and pepper, to taste
fresh parsley, for garnish

Bring the leeks, potatoes and water to a boil. Salt lightly, cover partially, and simmer 20-30 minutes, or until the vegetables are tender. Purée the soup; taste, and correct seasoning. After chilling the soup, you may wish to stir in a little more cream. Top each serving with a sprinkle of parsley. Serves six.

SALADES

GUSTAVE'S CAESAR SALAD

1 head romaine lettuce
3/4 cup extra virgin olive oil
3 tablespoons red wine vinegar
1 teaspoon Worcestershire sauce
1/2 teaspoon salt
1/4 tablespoon ground mustard
1 clove crushed garlic
l egg
1 lemon, juiced
freshly-ground pepper, to taste
1/4 cup grated Parmesan cheese
1 1/2 cups garlic croutons
1 (2-ounce) can anchovy filets

Clean romaine thoroughly and wrap in paper towels to absorb moisture. Refrigerate until crisp, at least 1 hour or more. In a bowl or jar combine oil, vinegar, Worcestershire sauce, salt, mustard, garlic and lemon juice. Whisk until well blended. Coddle egg by heating 3 cups of water to boiling. Drop in egg (still in shell) and let stand for 1 minute. Remove egg from water and let cool. Once cooled crack open and whisk egg into dressing. Whisk until thoroughly blended. Mash desired amount of anchovies and whisk them into the dressing. If desired set aside a few for garnish. To assemble, place torn romaine leaves in a large bowl. Pour dressing over the top and toss lightly. Add the grated cheese, garlic croutons and freshly ground pepper, toss. Serves four.

HEARTS OF LETTUCE

1 head lettuce
1 tablespoon chopped chives
1 tablespoon chopped parsley
Roquefort dressing (page 10)

Remove outside leaves and core from lettuce; wash and drain. Cut lengthwise into quarters; arrange each on a salad plate; sprinkle with chives and parsley, and serve with dressing. Serves four.

SHRIMP SALAD

2 cups cooked shrimp, halved lengthwise and chilled
1 cup thinly sliced celery
1 tablespoon finely minced onion
1 tablespoon fresh lemon juice
1/2 cup mayonnaise
salt and pepper, to taste
romaine lettuce or mixed greens
2 tomatoes, thinly sliced
A few slices freshly cooked bacon, crumbled (optional)

Combine shrimp with celery, onion, lemon juice, mayonnaise, and salt and pepper to taste. Arrange lettuce leaves on serving plates; top with thinly sliced tomatoes. Arrange shrimp over lettuce and tomatoes. If desired, garnish each with a little crumbled bacon. Serves four.

CRAB LOUIS

1 large crab
1 cup mayonnaise
1/4 cup heavy cream
1/4 cup chili sauce
1/4 cup chopped green pepper
1/4 cup chopped green onion
2 tablespoons chopped green olives
salt, to taste
lemon juice
1 tomato, for garnish
1 egg, hard boiled, for garnish

Arrange the crab meat in a bed of lettuce. Pour over it the dressing and garnish it with the crab legs, quartered tomatoes, and quartered hard boiled eggs, arranged symmetrically. Serves two.

REYNAUD'S CHEF SALAD

8 cups salad greens, washed and torn into bite sized pieces
1 cup ham, julienne strips
1 cup turkey, julienne strips

1/2 cup green onion, chopped fine
1/2 cup celery, chopped fine
1 cup cherry tomatoes, halved
1/2 cup Swiss cheese, julienne strips
1/2 cup cheddar cheese, julienne strips
2 eggs, hard boiled, peeled and sliced
1/4 cup chopped bacon, for garnish
8 ounces salad dressing, of your choice

Wash and tear salad greens into bite sized pieces; place in a large bowl. Toss with remaining ingredients, reserving some julienned pieces of meat and cheese for garnish. Just before serving, toss with a dressing of your choice and garnish with strips of meat, cheese and hard cooked egg slices. Serves six.

WALDORF SALAD

6 red-skinned apples
1 cup chopped celery
1 cup coarsely-chopped walnuts or pecans
1 cup mayonnaise
2 tablespoons lemon juice
6 lettuce cups

Wash, dry and polish the apples. Cut in quarters and core quarter but do not peel. Cut each quarter into 1/2-inch cubes, and toss with celery and nuts. Combine mayonnaise and lemon juice. Add to apple mixture and stir to mix well. Serve in individual lettuce "cups." Serves six.

HEARTS OF PALM

1/3 cup salad oil
1 teaspoon sugar
1/2 teaspoon aromatic bitters
2 tablespoon finely chopped stuffed green olives
1 (14-ounce) can hearts of palm, drained, sliced
2 tablespoon lemon juice
1/2 teaspoon salt
1/4 teaspoon paprika
1 tablespoon finely chopped onion
1 tablespoon finely chopped celery
6 cups torn Bibb lettuce

Combine salad oil, lemon juice, sugar, salt, bitters, paprika, olives, onion, and celery; beat well. Chill. At serving time toss together hearts of palm and lettuce in salad bowl. Add dressing and toss. Serves six.

ROQUEFORT DRESSING

1 1/2 cups mayonnaise
1/3 cup buttermilk
1/4 cup sour cream
2 tablespoons fresh lemon juice
1/2 teaspoon Worcestershire sauce
1/4 teaspoon Tabasco sauce
1 cup Roquefort cheese, crumbled coarsely
salt and pepper, to taste

In a bowl, whisk together all ingredients except Roquefort until smooth and then stir in cheese. Season with salt and pepper.

RUSSIAN DRESSING

1 cup mayonnaise
1/2 cup sour cream
1/2 cup ketchup
2 tablespoons grated onion
1/2 teaspoon ground dry mustard
4 dashes hot sauce
1 teaspoon Worcestershire sauce
2 tablespoons heavy cream
2 tablespoons minced fresh parsley

In a medium bowl, whisk together the mayonnaise, sour cream, ketchup, onion, mustard, hot sauce, Worcestershire, cream and parsley until smooth. Chill overnight to let ingredients incorporate.

ENTREES

POACHED KENNEBEC SALMON STEAK À LA MORTON DOWNEY

1 pound fresh salmon steak
3 tablespoons mayonnaise

Cut the salmon into slices about one inch thick and poach them in a court bouillon. Let the slices on a round dish. Garnish the dish with fresh vegetables cut in small pieces and covered with mayonnaise (slices tomato, half hard-boiled egg, etc.). Serves two.

(Mr. Reynaud explains that "court bouillon" is one sliced carrot, one sliced onion, four teaspoons vinegar, bay leaf, whole black pepper, and water, boiled together). Serves one.

FROG LEGS SAUTÈ SALONAISE

10 medium frog legs
1/2 cup heavy cream
salt and pepper, to taste
4 tablespoons flour
2 tablespoons olive oil
1 onion
1/2 eggplant
1 tomato
1 clove of garlic, finely chopped
lemon wedges

Dip the frog legs in cream and season. Roll in flour and fry in hot olive oil until golden brown. Sauté onions, diced egg plant, chopped fresh tomatoes. Cook for ten minutes and add garlic which has been cooked in butter. Pour over frog legs. Serve with lemon. Serves two.

ESCARGOTS BOURGUIGNONNE

12 snails
2 ounces garlic
1 ounce shallots
salt and pepper, to taste
1 ounce Pernod
1 ounce fresh parsley
10 ounces butter
dry white wine

Chop garlic, parsley, and shallots. Add 1 ounce of Pernod. Adjust seasonings. Add the butter and mix in well. Boil the live snails in their shells in salted water for 10 minutes; remove from shells. Stuff the shells with the garlic, parsley, shallots and butter mixture. Put the snails back into the shells and put more of the mixture on top of them. Place the shells on a baking dish, propping up the shells with coarse sand so that the opening of the shell is on top. Place in an oven at 350-degrees just until the butter begins to sizzle. Remove and sprinkle with the wine. Serves two.

FILET OF SOLE SAUTE AMANDINE

1/2 pound sole fillet
2 tablespoons butter
1 tablespoon almonds, blanched, slivered
1 lemon wedge
fresh parsley

Sauté sole over low flame in butter. Transfer to heated platter. Very quickly fry almonds in remaining butter (raise flame under pan). Pour hot butter and almonds over fish and garnish with lemon and parsley. Serves one.

BROILED SHRIMPS PROVENÇALE

2 pounds jumbo shrimps
1/4 cup olive oil
2 cloves garlic, finely chopped
2 teaspoons each fresh oregano, rosemary and marjoram
1 cup chopped tomato
1/2 cup white wine
salt and pepper, to taste

Season both slices of fish and moisten with olive oil. Place remaining olive oil and ingredients into a shallow ovenproof baking dish just large enough to hold the fillets. Broil for 10 minutes. Serves four.

BROILED BLUEFISH SHERMAN

2 pounds bluefish
1 cup mayonnaise
1/2 cup Old Bay seasoning
soy sauce

Place fish in shallow baking pan. Spread mayonnaise over each piece of fish. Sprinkle Old Bay seasoning over mayonnaise. Shake soy sauce on top and broil in oven until brown, about 15 minutes, 400-degrees. Serves four.

BROILED POMPANO TYROLIENNE

4 pompano fillets
salt and pepper, to taste
Tyrolienne sauce (page 96)

Season the pompano fillets with salt and pepper and place under the broiler for about 3 minutes per side, or until just cooked through. Spoon Tyrolienne sauce over the top. Serves four.

CURRY OF JUMBO SHRIMPS WITH WILD RICE

1 large onion, quartered
1 (2-inch-long) piece fresh ginger, peeled
1/2 teaspoon salt
1/2 teaspoon sugar
1/4 cup vegetable oil
1 1/2 teaspoons curry powder
1 to 2 fresh serrano chiles, halved
1 cup water
1 (14-ounce) can unsweetened coconut milk
1 tablespoon fresh lime juice
1 pound large shrimp in shell

Chop onion and ginger and cook with salt and sugar in oil in a skillet, stirring frequently, until onion begins to brown, about 5 minutes. Stir in curry powder and chiles and cook, stirring frequently, 2 minutes. Stir in water, coconut milk, and lime juice and simmer, stirring occasionally, until thickened, 5 to 8 minutes. While sauce simmers, peel shrimp (devein if desired) and season with salt and pepper. Add shrimp to sauce and simmer, stirring occasionally, until shrimp are just cooked through, about 3 minutes. Add salt to taste and serve with cooked wild rice. Serves four.

SOLE WELLINGTON

1 sheet puff pastry
2 tablespoons butter
1/2 cup diced sweet onions
4 ounces coarse-chopped mushrooms
2 garlic cloves, pressed
salt and pepper, to taste
2 tablespoons chopped fresh parsley
4 ounces cream cheese, at room temperature
1 tablespoons Dijon mustard
1/2 teaspoons dried thyme leaves, crushed
4 sole fillets
1 large egg, beaten with 1 teaspoon water for an egg wash

Melt butter in skillet and sauté onions, mushrooms, garlic, and salt and pepper to taste. Stir in parsley and set aside to cool. Mix cream cheese, Dijon mustard, thyme, and sage. Set aside. Roll out puff pastry and cut into 4 squares. Divide cream cheese mixture equally amongst the squares, then top with mushroom mixture, and chilled chicken chunks or strips. Brush edges with egg wash. Bring corners of the pastry square to the center, sealing all edges to contain the filling. Bake for 25 minutes until golden brown. Serves four.

LOBSTER NEWBURG

1 1/2 pounds steamed lobster tails
4 tablespoons butter
paprika
3 tablespoons flour
1 cup cream
salt and pepper, to taste
1/2 cup dry sherry wine
Melba toast

Dice lobster meat and sauté lightly in butter. Add paprika to taste, stir, then blend in flour until cooked, not brown. Add 2/3 cup warm cream, stir until thick. Season with salt and pepper. Remove from fire, add remaining cream, stir. Add wine and stir. Pour into warm casserole; sprinkle with paprika. Heat in broiler or hot oven. Serve with Melba toast. Serves four.

LOBSTER THERMADOR

2 cups cream sauce
salt, pepper, and paprika, to taste
1/2 teaspoon mustard
2 tablespoons sherry wine
2 egg yolks
1 pound chopped lobster meat

Make 2 cups of cream sauce and season with salt, pepper, paprika and mustard. Add the wine. Beat the egg yolks well and add slowly to the hot cream sauce. Add chopped lobster meat and mix together thoroughly. Pour mixture into lobster shell and bake in hot oven until golden brown. Serves four.

BROILED CALF'S LIVER

8 ounces sliced bacon
2 tablespoons olive oil
4 medium sweet onions, halved root-to-stem and thinly sliced
1 pound calf's liver, sliced in half horizontally
salt and pepper, to taste

Sauté bacon until crispy. Sauté until onions are very soft and beginning to brown. Season liver with salt and pepper to taste, and broil as desired. To serve, place a slice of liver on each of two serving plates. Smother with onions and top with bacon. Serves two.

CALVES LIVER SAUTÈ LYONNAISE

4 slices calves liver
salt and pepper, to taste
3 tablespoons butter

Cut the liver into slices, weighting two ounces each. Toss in hot butter until golden brown. Season. Arrange the slices in a circle in a round silver platter and in the center garnish with Lyonnaise potatoes (page 78). Serves two.

STEAK TARTARE BETTE DAVIS

1 pound tenderloin steak, finely ground
1 teaspoon brown mustard
1/2 teaspoon Tabasco
1 teaspoon Worcestershire sauce
1 teaspoon brandy
1 pinch salt, or to taste
ground white pepper to taste
1 egg

In a medium bowl, mix together the beef, mustard, hot pepper sauce, Worcestershire, brandy, salt, pepper and egg until well blended. Arrange the meat in a neat pile on a glass dish, and cover. Refrigerate for 30 minutes to allow the flavors to blend. Serve as a spread on crackers or toast. Serves four.

WALTER WINCHELL BURGER

1 pound ground white meat chicken
2 cups coarse bread crumbs
1/2 cup heavy cream
3 tablespoons grated sweet onion, minced
1/4 teaspoon nutmeg
3/4 teaspoon coarse grained salt
salt and pepper, to taste
1 tablespoon butter
tomato sauce

Place chicken in a mixing bowl. Using a rubber spatula, fold in milk, 1/2 cup bread crumbs, onion, cayenne, salt and pepper. Place remaining 1 1/2 cups bread crumbs on a dinner plate or cookie sheet. Divide chicken meat into 4 patties. Coat each patty with bread crumbs. Heat olive oil in a large non-stick skillet over medium heat and fry patties until golden and cooked through, about 5 minutes per side. Serve with a side of sweet potato fries (see page 76) and buttered green peas. Serves four.

MINUTE STEAK CHEZ TOI

4 (1/2 pound) top-round minute steaks, cut into serving-size pieces salt
    and pepper, to taste

Using a kitchen mallet, thoroughly score or pound the surface of the meat. Scoring and pounding will help the juices contained in the meat to release more easily during the cooking time, which will result in the minute steak remaining moist and supple when it arrives at the dinner table. After pounding the steak and infusing it with salt and pepper, place the steak in a pre-heated frying pan and sear for a moment on each side. Add a dash of soy sauce at this stage, if desired. Serve with diced potatoes, glazed onions and mushrooms. Serves four.

FILET MIGNON ROUMANILLE

1/2 pound filet mignon
Mornay sauce
pitted olives, chopped
filet of anchovy

Grill the filet mignon for five minutes on each side. Cover with Mornay sauce (page 92) and brown. Place olives and filet of anchovy on top. Serve on a round platter, placing around filet mignon diced mushrooms, half-boiled fresh tomato, a slice of egg plant, and Parisienne potatoes (page 77). Serves two.

FILET MIGNON CAPUCINE

2 tenderloin steaks
1 tablespoon melted butter mixed with 1 teaspoon vegetable oil

Brush tops of steaks with oil and butter and broil 4 minutes a side for rare; turn over, brush other side with butter or oil and broil 4 minutes a side (cook 5 to 7 minutes a side for medium rare; never cook until well done). Serve with Bernaise Sauce (page 95), French onions (page 74), and creamed spinach (page 69). Serves two.

STEAK DIANE

2 club steaks, 8 ounces each, cut 1/4-inch thick
1 teaspoon dry mustard
2 tablespoons A.l. Sauce
4 tablespoons butter
2 tablespoons warm cognac
4 tablespoons sherry wine
1 tablespoon chopped chives

Rub the steaks with a mixture of the mustard and A.l. Sauce. Melt 2 tablespoons butter in a skillet. Add the steaks and cook over high heat 2 minutes on each side. Set the cognac aflame in a ladle and pour over the steaks. Immediately add the sherry, chives, and remaining butter. Transfer the steaks to a hot serving dish, bring the sauce to a boil, and pour over the steaks. Serves two.

PRIME BEEF STEW WITH FRESH VEGETABLES

2 pounds prime beef, cut into cubes
2 tablespoons vegetable oil
2 cups water
1 tablespoon Worcestershire
1 clove garlic
2 bay leaves
1 onion, sliced
salt and pepper, to taste
1/2 teaspoon paprika
3 carrots, sliced
3 stalks celery, chopped
2 tablespoons cornstarch

Brown meat in hot oil. Add water, Worcestershire sauce, garlic, bay leaves, onion, salt, pepper, and paprika. Cover and simmer 1 1/2 hours. Remove bay leaves and garlic clove. Add carrots and celery. Cover and cook 30 to 40 minutes longer. To thicken gravy, remove 2 cups hot liquid. Using a separate bowl, combine 1/4 cup water and cornstarch until smooth. Mix with a little hot liquid and return mixture to pot. Serves six.

ESCALLOPED SWEETBREADS GRAN DUE

4 sweetbreads
6 tablespoons butter
1/4 pound mushroom caps
Mornay sauce
salt and pepper, to taste

Boil the sweetbreads for about five minutes, then cool. Cut into slices, season, and cook in butter, stirring constantly. Dish them in the form of a crown, placing slices of sauteed mushrooms and Mornay sauce (page 81) between each coat, and glaze quickly in hot oven. Remove from oven, arrange a heap of asparagus heads covered with butter in the center of the dish and serve at once. Serves four.

CURRIED LAMB A L'INDIENNE

2 pounds lean lamb
4 tablespoons lard
1 onion
salt
2 tablespoons powdered curry
3 tablespoons flour
1 1/3 cups water or stock
2 cups boiled rice

Cut lamb into cubes and fry in hot grease with chopped onion, salt and powdered curry. When the meat is well browned and the onions begin to color, sprinkle with flour, cook until flour blends, then moisten with water or stock. Boil, stirring frequently, and place in moderate oven for one and one-half hours. Remove all grease before serving. Serve with boiled rice. Serves four.

STORK COMBINATION HASH

2 large russet potatoes, peeled and cut into 1/2-inch cubes
1/2 teaspoon salt
1/4 teaspoon black pepper
1/4 cup butter or margarine
1 large onion, chopped
1/2 pound corned beef, finely chopped
1 tablespoon horseradish
1/4 cup heavy cream
4 poached or fried eggs

Boil potatoes, drain, and season with salt and pepper. Add butter and onion to a skillet and cook for 5 minutes. Stir in corned beef, horseradish and potatoes; mix well. Press down mixture with spatula to flatten into compact layer. Drizzle cream evenly over mixture. Cook 10 minutes on each side. Top each serving with 1 poached or fried egg. Serves four.

CHICKEN POT PIE

1/3 cup butter or margarine
1/3 cup chopped onion
1/3 cup all-purpose flour
1/2 teaspoon salt
1/4 teaspoon pepper
1 3/4 cups chicken broth
1/2 cup milk
2 1/2 cups shredded cooked chicken or turkey
2 cups mixed vegetables, chopped

Melt butter in a skillet and add onion; cook 2 minutes, stirring frequently, until tender. Stir in flour, salt and pepper until well blended. Gradually stir in broth and milk, cooking and stirring until bubbly and thickened. Stir in chicken and mixed vegetables. Remove from heat. Spoon chicken mixture into pie crust-lined pan. Top with second crust; seal edge and flute. Cut slits in several places in top crust. Bake 30 to 40 minutes or until crust is golden brown. Let stand 5 minutes before serving. Serves four.

FRIED CHICKEN LOUISIANA

2 1/2 pound chicken
1/2 cup heavy cream
4 tablespoon butter salt and pepper, to taste
1 cantaloupe
2 cups whole kernel corn
green pepper
pimento

Cut the chicken in six pieces. Dip each piece in cream and season. Fry in butter. Cut a cantaloupe in half and remove meat.[*] Heat shell in oven. Saute corn with green pepper and pimento and partially fill cantaloupe shell. Place chicken on top, garnish wish candied sweet potatoes, and serve. Serves two.

BREAST OF CAPON LOUELLA PARSONS

4 breasts of capon
4 slices Virginia or smoked ham
4 mushroom caps
4 cups cream sauce
1 cup cream
3 ounces sherry wine

---

[*] Use the cantaloupe meat for a melon cocktail.

In melted butter, sauté the capon breasts face down on slow fire until brown. Repeat on other side for 10 minutes or until done. Remove capons and sauté mushrooms and ham, then remove from pan. Pour wine into the pan and reduce for 5 minutes. Add the cream sauce and cream and simmer for 5 minutes. Serve capons, ham and mushrooms on toast covered with the sauce. Serves four.

STUFFED SQUAB DAMON RUNYON

2 boneless squabs
1/4 pound wild rice
1 small onion, finely chopped
1 bay leaf
1 small piece celery
1/4 pound fresh butter
1 pint chicken stock
4 fried chopped chicken livers
2 teaspoons chopped chives
4 ounces sherry wine

Bake rice in oven with onion, bay leaf, celery, butter and chicken stock for 20 minutes. When done, add chicken livers and mix with chives and 2 ounces of sherry. Stuff squabs and bake in oven 20 minutes or more until done. Remove squabs from pan and glacé the pan with a little sherry and a little chicken stock. Allow it to reduce somewhat and serve, pouring sauce over the top. Serves two.

QUAIL À LA JANE RUSSELL

4 quail
4 small white onions
4 cubes salt pork
1 ½ teaspoons salt
½ teaspoon pepper
pinch nutmeg
1 bay leaf
4 tablespoons butter
3 tablespoons A.l. Sauce

In each bird, place one onion and one piece of salt pork. Truss, then rub with a mixture of the salt, pepper, nutmeg, bay leaf, 2 tablespoons butter, and 1 tablespoon A.l. Sauce. Arrange in a shallow buttered baking pan, add the remaining butter and A.l. Sauce. Bake in oven for 30 minutes, until tender and browned. Baste frequently. Transfer the quail to heated serving dishes and pour pan juices over them. Serves two.

LAMB CHOPS A LA MURILLO

4 lamb chops
4 mushroom caps
4 tablespoons cream sauce
4 tablespoons grated cheese
2 tablespoons butter
1 green pepper
1 large tomato

Fry the chops in butter on only one side. Garnish the cooked side, dome fashion, with a fine hash of sautéed mushrooms mixed with very thick cream sauce. Set them on a baking tray, sprinkle with grated cheese and melted butter and glaze in a very hot oven. Fix a frill to each chop and serve in the form of a crown. Surround the chops with sliced green pepper and tomatoes, tossed in butter. Serves two.

SMOKED TURKEY WITH BROCCOLI MORNAY

1 bunch of broccoli
1 pound cooked turkey
Mornay sauce (page 92)
4 tablespoons grated cheese

On a round platter, place a bunch of cooked broccoli. On the broccoli place a layer of turkey, alternating white and dark meat. Pour Mornay sauce on top of turkey, sprinkle with grated cheese and brown in oven. Serves two.

DUCK A LA DIETRICH

4 breasts of duck
1/2 pint beef stock
4 half peaches, poached in red wine
1 ounce butter.
1 tablespoon vegetable oil
salt and pepper, to taste

Fry breasts on high heat turning once, season and lower heat cooking gently until golden brown. Remove breasts and keep warm. Drain the duck fat from the pan, add stock to pan and stir with remains, heat, add peach syrup (liquid only), whisk in the cold butter. Cut breast in diagonal slices, serve sauce around breast, not on top. Decorate dish with peach halves. Serve remaining sauce separately. Serves four.

POTATOES AND VEGETABLES

ASPARAGUS À LA STORK

1 bunch asparagus
3 ounces Parmesan cheese
2 tablespoons butter, melted

Boil asparagus until tender, drain and arrange in successive rows. Sprinkle the heads of each row with grated Parmesan. Just before serving cover the heads generously with melted butter and glaze slightly. Serve with fried or poached eggs on slices of broiled Virginia ham. Serves two.

CREAMED SPINACH

1/4 cup finely chopped onion
3/4 cup heavy cream
24 ounces baby spinach, washed
salt and pepper, to taste

Combine onions and cream. Simmer until cream is reduced by half and thickened and onion is soft, about 10 minutes. Cook spinach in a dry pot, stirring occasionally, until wilted. Drain and return the pot to the stove. Add the reduced cream mixture and stir to combine. Season well with salt and pepper. Serves six.

STEWED TOMATOES

2 pounds tomatoes, peeled, cut into pieces
1 teaspoon salt
1/8 teaspoon pepper
2 teaspoons sugar
1 tablespoon butter
1 tablespoon finely minced onion, optional

Place tomatoes in a medium saucepan; cover tightly. Cook tomatoes over lowest heat for about 15 minutes, stirring occasionally. Add the salt, pepper, sugar, and butter, along with minced onion and green pepper, if using. Simmer for 10 to 15 minutes, stirring frequently, until juices are slightly reduced. Serves four.

GLAZED CARROTS

4 medium carrots
2 tablespoons butter
2 tablespoons sugar
mint leaves, optional

Wash and scrape carrots. Cook in boiling salted water until tender. Drain. Cut in slices. Melt butter. Add sugar. Add carrots. Cook until slightly browned and glazed. Add a teaspoon of chopped fresh mint leaves to the butter and sugar mixture, if desired. Serves four.

BROCCOLI AND CHEESE

16 ounces broccoli spears
12 ounces American cheese, shredded
2/3 cup milk
1/2 teaspoon onion powder
dash ground cayenne or hot pepper sauce, if desired
salt and pepper, to taste

Prepare broccoli in a steamer. Combine remaining ingredients. Heat, stirring frequently, until cheese is melted and mixture is smooth, about 7 minutes. Season with salt and pepper, as desired. Pour sauce over broccoli arranged on a serving platter or in a bowl, or serve sauce separately. Serves six.

BRAISED SAVOY CABBAGE

1 medium Savoy cabbage, washed
2 cloves garlic, chopped
1/2 cup apple cider vinegar
1/2 cup chicken stock
2 tablespoons butter
olive oil
salt

Remove outer green leaves of the cabbage. Cut into quarters, remove the heart, and slice crosswise into fine ribbons. In an oiled saute pan, add garlic and cook until slightly transparent. Add the butter and cabbage and sauté for 3 minutes, stirring constantly. Season lightly with salt, and then add the apple cider vinegar to deglaze. Add the chicken stock and cook until the cabbage is tender and the liquid has reduced. Serves four.

FRENCH ONIONS

1/2 pound onions
2 tablespoons butter
1 teaspoon sugar
1 1/2 teaspoons flour
1/4 cup milk
1/2 cup fat-skimmed beef broth

1/2 cup shredded gruyère cheese
2 tablespoons grated parmesan cheese
salt and pepper, to taste

Peel and thinly slice onion. In a frying pan, combine onion, butter, sugar. Stir until onion is limp and lightly browned. Add flour and mix well. Remove pan from heat; stir in milk and beef broth. Stir until boiling; continue stirring until liquid is almost evaporated and mixture doesn't flow when scraped from pan bottom. Remove from heat. Add gruyère cheese and parmesan cheese; stir until melted. Season with salt and pepper. Serves four.

POTATOES AU GRATIN

1/4 cup (1/2 stick) butter or margarine
1/4 cup flour
1 teaspoon salt
1/2 teaspoon dry mustard
1/4 teaspoon pepper
2 1/2 cups milk
8 ounces shredded Cheddar cheese
2 tablespoons chopped onion
6 cups peeled potatoes, thinly sliced

Melt butter in saucepan and blend in flour, salt, mustard and pepper. Gradually add milk, stirring until well blended; cook until thickened, stirring constantly. 1 1/2 cups of the cheese and the onion; cook until cheese is melted, stirring frequently. Layer potatoes and cheese sauce alternately in casserole dish. Bake 1 hour, until potatoes are tender. Sprinkle with the remaining cheese and bake an additional 5 minutes. Serves four.

SWEET POTATO FRIES

1 1/2 pounds sweet potatoes
2 tablespoons crushed rosemary
salt, to taste

Wash sweet potatoes and cut into long thin strips, about 1/4 inch thick. Place in ice water for about 15 minutes. Preheat deep fryer. Remove sweet potato fries from water and pat dry with paper towels· Place in hot oil about 350 degrees. Fry for about 5 minute of until golden brown. Remove from oil and allow to drain.

PARISIENNE POTATOES

3 pounds potatoes, peeled
3 tablespoons extra-virgin olive oil
3 tablespoons butter
4 garlic cloves, minced
salt and pepper, to taste
parsley, chopped for garnish

Using a melon baller, make small potato balls, 5 to 7 are needed per person. They can be made in advance and kept in cold water. Place potato balls in a saucepan covering them completely in cold water, bring to a boil then drain. Heat the olive oil and butter in a skillet over medium heat, add the potato balls, minced garlic, salt and pepper. Shake or stir the pan occasionally to ensure even cooking, do not burn the garlic. Test for doneness with the tip of a sharp knife. Serves six.

LYONNAISE POTATOES

olive oil
2 large russet potatoes, peeled and sliced
1 large yellow onion, thinly sliced
1/3 cup chicken stock

Lightly coat a small baking pan with olive oil. Layer potatoes and onion in pan. Season with salt and pepper. Pour stock over potatoes and onion; cover and bake 30 minutes in a 350-degree oven. Lightly spray or brush with olive oil and return to oven, uncovered, 10 more minutes to lightly brown potatoes. Serves four.

EGG DISHES

CHEESE SOUFFLÈ DER BINGLE

3 tablespoons butter
1 cup flour
5 eggs
2 1/2 cups milk
salt and pepper, to taste
pinch nutmeg
1/2 pound Parmesan cheese

Mix melted butter, flour and beaten egg yolks. Add boiling milk gradually. Season with salt, pepper and nutmeg and cook slowly, stirring constantly. When the sauce reaches a boil, remove from flame and add grated Parmesan cheese. Run the mixture through a sieve and then fold into egg-whites which have been whisked to a stiff froth. Mold in a baking dish lined with buttered paper and bake in hot oven for twenty to twenty-five minutes. Serves three.

SCRAMBLED EGGS GEORGETTE

2 medium-sized Idaho potatoes
4 eggs
4 tablespoons cream
salt and pepper, to taste
4 shrimps, chopped
Parsley

Bake the potatoes and withdraw the inside pulp[*], making as small incision as possible at the top. Keep remaining shell hot. Scramble the eggs with cream and season. Add chopped shrimps and chopped parsley. Serves two.

SCRAMBLED EGGS DIVETTE

4 eggs
1 tablespoon butter
2 tablespoons cream
salt and pepper, to taste
1/4 pound Louisiana shrimps, sliced
1/2 cup asparagus tips

Sauté the asparagus tips in the butter and set aside. Scramble the eggs with cream and season. Add the shrimps and asparagus. Serves two.

OMELETTE STEVE HANNAGAN

3 eggs
butter
salt and pepper, to taste
2 tablespoons mushrooms, diced and sauteed
2 tablespoons eggplant, diced and fried
2 tablespoons stewed tomatoes

Put frying pan over a low heat and put in at least 2 to 3 level tablespoons of butter. Break the eggs into a mixing bowl, adjust seasonings, then add a tablespoon of water. Beat the eggs with a fork for 25 to 30 seconds or about 45 strokes. Turn the heat to medium high, and when the butter is a nice light brown in color, give the eggs a final quick beating and pour them into the pan. Quickly move the

---

[*] Potato pulp may be served at side.

eggs from the outer edges of the pan to the center with a fork so the liquid keeps running under and cooking. In about 5 seconds an envelope will form on the omelette. Place the fillings in the middle and fold inside the omelette. Serves one.

SHIRRED EGGS BIBESCO

1 tablespoon butter
2 tablespoons olive oil
salt and pepper, to taste
1 pound tongue, julienne
1/4 cup chopped mushrooms
1 1/4 ounce Perigordine truffles, finely chopped
9 large eggs
1/4 cup bread crumbs
1/4 cup grated Parmigiano cheese
Madeira sauce (see page 94)

Preheat the oven to 400 degrees. Butter 4 individual oval au gratin ramekins and place on a baking sheet. Heat the olive oil in a sauté pan and add the tongue. Adjust seasonings. Sauté for 2 minutes. Add the mushrooms and continue to sauté for 2 minutes. Add the truffles. Sauté for 1 minute. Remove the mixture from the heat and allow to cool in a mixing bowl. Add one of the eggs, bread crumbs and cheese and mix well. Spread 1/4 of the filling over the bottom of each ramekin. Crack two eggs over each ramekin of filling. Place the ramekins in the oven and cook for about 6 to 8 minutes, or until the white of the eggs are firm but the yolks are still liquid. Remove from the oven and place on individual serving plates. Serves four.

OMELETTE GLORIA VANDERBILT

1 tablespoon butter
3 eggs slightly beaten
3 tablespoon chopped watercress leaves
1/4 teaspoon salt
1/8 teaspoon pepper
1/4 cup sour cream
2 tablespoons red or black caviar

Melt butter in skillet over moderate heat. Combine eggs, watercress, salt and pepper then add to pan. Cook lifting edges with fork until omelet is done then fold omelet in half. Turn out onto serving plate then top with sour cream and caviar.

EGGS EVA GABOR

6 sausages, sliced
4 eggs
1/2 cup cream
3/4 teaspoon salt
1/4 cup finely chopped green pepper
2 tablespoons butter

Brown the sausages in a skillet. Drain well and discard the fat. Beat the eggs, cream, and salt. Mix in the green pepper. Melt the butter in the skillet, and lightly scramble the eggs in it. Fold in the sausages and serve. Serves two

SAUCES

MORNAY SAUCE

4 tablespoons butter
4 tablespoons flour
4 cups milk
salt, to taste
pinch nutmeg
bay leaf
2 egg yolks

Melt butter and flour, keeping sauce very white. Cool. Gradually add boiled milk, stirring constantly, and season with salt, nutmeg, and bay leaf. Bring to a boil, then cook very slowly for one hour. Strain through a sieve and add beaten egg yolks to mixture gradually.

CHEESE SAUCE

4 tablespoons butter
1/2 cup flour
3 cups milk
salt and pepper, to taste
8 tablespoons grated cheddar cheese

Melt the butter, add the flour, and cook 5 minutes. Heat the milk slightly, but do not scald. Gradually add it to the butter and flour. Stir and cook until smooth, 15 to 20 minutes. Add the salt, pepper, and cheese. Stir until the cheese is melted and the mixture is smooth.

MADEIRA SAUCE

3 tablespoons finely chopped shallots
1 ounce butter
1/2 pound white or crimini mushrooms
1/2 teaspoon cracked peppercorn
1 bay leaf
1/4 teaspoon dried thyme
1/4 cup red wine
3/4 cup Madeira wine
1 cup demi-glace
1/4 cup heavy cream

Sauté shallots in butter for 1–2 minutes. Add mushrooms and cook until mushrooms are tender. Remove mushrooms and set aside.

Add peppercorns, thyme, and bay leaf and cook 30 seconds. Add red wine and reduce by half. Add Madeira wine and bring to boil. Add demi-glace and whisk until incorporated into the sauce. Return mushrooms to pan and stir in heavy cream.

BERNAISE SAUCE

1/2 cup white wine vinegar
5 shallots, minced
2 tablespoons minced fresh tarragon
1/2 teaspoon white pepper
4 egg yolks
1/2 cup boiling water
1 cup warm clarified butter
salt, to taste

Combine vinegar, shallots, 1 tablespoon tarragon, and pepper in saucepan. Bring to boil and cook, stirring constantly until liquid is almost totally evaporated. Remove from heat and let cool. Add egg yolks, beating constantly with wire whisk. Add the water and blend well. Heat the sauce again, beating constantly. When sauce has become creamy, remove from heat and let cool. Add clarified butter gradually, beating gently. Strain sauce through sieve. Season with salt and remaining tarragon and chervil. Sauce should have consistency of mayonnaise.

TYROLIENNE SAUCE

1 cup mayonnaise
1 tablespoon chopped parsley
1 tablespoon chopped chervil
1/4 cup chopped tomatoes

1/8 teaspoon black pepper
1/4 teaspoon Worcestershire sauce
1 teaspoon chili sauce

Heat and reduce the chopped tomatoes to a thick consistency. Cool tomatoes, and combine with all ingredients.

MEUNIÈRE SAUCE

3/4 cup butter
2 tablespoons chopped green onions
3 tablespoons lemon juice
1 dash hot pepper sauce
1 teaspoon minced parsley
salt and pepper, to taste
1 dash Worcestershire sauce

Combine all ingredients and simmer 5 minutes.

CHINESE SPECIALTIES

CHOP SUEY

1/4 cup shortening
1 1/2 cups diced pork loin
1 cup diced onion
1 cup diced celery
1 cup hot water
1 teaspoon salt
1/8 teaspoon ground black pepper
1 (14-ounce) can bean sprouts, drained and rinsed
1/3 cup cold water
2 tablespoons cornstarch
2 teaspoons soy sauce
1 teaspoon white sugar

Heat shortening in a large, deep skillet. Sear pork until it turns white, then add onion and saute for 5 minutes. Add celery, hot water, salt and pepper. Cover skillet and simmer for 5 minutes. Add sprouts and heat to boiling. In a small bowl combine the cold water, cornstarch, soy sauce and sugar. Mix together and add to skillet mixture. Cook for 5 minutes, or until thickened to taste. Serves four.

SHRIMP CHOW MEIN

1 pound fresh shelled shrimp
1/4 cup soy sauce
2 tablespoons cornstarch
2 chicken bouillon cubes
1 cup boiling water
3 tablespoons vegetable oil
1 small onion, chopped
1/2 cup sliced fresh mushrooms
1 garlic clove, minced
1 (16-ounce) can bean sprouts, drained
1 (8-ounce) can water chestnuts, drained and sliced
6 to 8 ounces broccoli
1/4 cup slivered almonds

Dissolve bouillon in boiling water, set aside. Mix soy sauce and cornstarch together and add to bouillon mixture. Set aside. In a preheated wok, swirl oil around sides. Stir-fry shrimp 6 to 8 minutes. Remove shrimp and set aside. Add remaining oil and stir-fry onion, mushroom and garlic for about 2 minutes. Remove and set aside. Add bean sprouts and water chestnuts and stir-fry for 1 minute. Add shrimp and onion mixture. Simmer 5 to 10 minutes. Serves four.

SUBGUM CHOW MEIN

3 cups diced cooked chicken
1/2 cup peanut oil
1 cup sliced water chestnuts
1 cup sliced bamboo shoots
3 cups sliced celery
2 cups sliced celery cabbage
1/4 pound pea pods
3/4 cup sliced mushrooms
1 large green pepper, sliced
9 scallions, chopped
2 garlic cloves, minced
1 tablespoon sugar
3 cups chicken bouillon
3 tablespoons cornstarch
1/4 cup soy sauce
1 tablespoon
salt and pepper, to taste
3/4 cup toasted almonds

In a pre-heated wok, swirl oil around sides. Add vegetables, sugar, salt and pepper, and stir-fry for 1 minute, stirring briskly. Add bouillon, bring to a boil, reduce heat, cover and simmer for 10 minutes. Combine cornstarch, soy sauce and 4 tablespoons water. Add to vegetable mixture and cook until thickened, stirring constantly. Add chicken and cook for 5 minutes. Serve garnished with almonds. Serves six.

MOO COO GAI PAN

3 boneless chicken breasts (cut up)
1/2 cup oil
3 slices ginger
2 garlic cloves
1 1/2 cups chicken stock (99% free works)
2 tablespoons cornstarch
1/2 lb sliced mushrooms
1/4 lb snow peas
1 (8-ounce) can water chestnuts (drained)
1 (8-ounce) can bamboo shoots (drained)
1/4 cup carrots (thin sticks)
4 green onions (sliced)
1/2 cup broccoli, florets (small)

In a pre-heated wok, swirl oil around sides. Add ginger and garlic. Brown and then discard. Add chicken and cook 4 minutes. Combine chicken stock and corn starch. Pour over chicken and reduce heat. Add all vegetables. Cover and simmer about 15 minutes. Season with soy sauce and serve over rice. Serves four.

FRIED RICE WITH BEEF

2 tablespoons soy sauce
1/2 teaspoon sugar
1 tablespoon vegetable oil
2 eggs, well beaten
1/2 pound beef, sliced
1 medium carrot, finely chopped
1 celery rib, finely chopped
1 scallion, chopped
1 teaspoon fresh ginger, minced
1 clove garlic, minced
2 cups cooked rice, cold

Combine soy sauce, sugar and salt and pepper to taste in a small bowl and set aside. In a pre-heated wok, swirl oil around sides. Cook eggs about 45 seconds, stirring constantly, until eggs are just set. Transfer eggs to a bowl and set aside. Add sliced beef and next 3 ingredients to same pan. Sauté about 3 minutes, stirring often to break up meat, until browned. Stir in ginger and garlic and cook 1 minute. Discard excess fat. Increase heat to high and add rice. Stir-fry about 1 minute, until heated through. Stir in soy sauce mixture and eggs and stir-fry 30 seconds longer. Serves four.

DESSERTS

COCONUT SNOWBALL

1 cup water
1/4 cup sugar
1 teaspoon vanilla
6 ounces (6 squares) unsweetened chocolate
6 scoops vanilla ice cream
1 can moist coconut shreds

Mix sugar and water in heavy saucepan. Add chocolate and cook over low heat, stirring constantly until chocolate is melted. Cool and add vanilla. (You can buy a number of good prepared chocolate syrups, if you haven't the time to make this special sauce.) On each plate, top a large scoop of vanilla ice cream with the chocolate sauce. Then snow it under with the shredded coconut. Serves six.

SOUFFLÈD OMELETTE VANILLA

4 egg yolks
1/2 cup sugar
1 teaspoon vanilla extract
5 egg whites
3 tablespoons confectioners sugar

Beat egg yolks and add sugar gradually until mixture has whitened slightly and draws up in ribbons when the spoon is drawn out of it. Add vanilla. Beat egg-whites to a very stiff froth and fold in the first mixture gently, cutting and rising the whole with a spoon. Mold on a long buttered and sugar-dusted dish in the shape of an oval mound, saving a small quantity aside to decorate the omelette. Smooth it all around with a knife. Decorate with portion of mixture from a piping-bag and bake in moderate oven. About two minutes before removing from oven, sprinkle it with icing sugar to form a brilliant coat when melted. Serves three.

CHERRIES JUBILEE

1/2 cup granulated sugar
1 tablespoon cornstarch
1/4 cup each water and orange juice
3 cups fresh sweet cherries, pitted
1/2 teaspoon grated orange peel
1/4 cup brandy, optional
1 quart vanilla ice cream

Combine sugar and cornstarch. Blend in water and orange juice. Cook and stir until thickened and smooth. Add cherries and orange peel; return to boil and simmer 10 minutes. Gently heat brandy, pour over sauce and flame, if desired. Serve over ice cream. Serves six.

BAKED ALASKA

1 layer sponge cake
1 quart ice cream
4 egg whites
1/2 cup sugar
1 teaspoon vanilla

Beat egg whites until nearly stiff, beat in sugar gradually, add vanilla and beat until stiff. Place a board at least 1 1/2 inches thick between 2 pieces of corrugated paper; cover top with waxed paper. Place round of sponge cake on board, heap ice cream quickly on top, leaving a 1-inch margin of cake all around; cover thickly with meringue. Brown quickly in very hot oven (450 degrees). Serves six.

CRÊPES SUZETTE

1/4 cup butter
2 cups orange marmalade
12 crepes
1/4 cup Cointreau
2 tablespoons brandy

Heat butter and marmalade in skillet until just bubbling. Add 1st crepe. Allow for sauce to cover both sides. Fold in half and then half again. Push folded crepe to side of pan and repeat with the remaining crepes. Sprinkle crepes with liquor and brandy. With a long match very carefully ignite pan. Carefully, spoon liquid over crepes in pan or rotate pan until flames go out. Serves six (2 crepes per person).

COUPE MONTMORENCY

Fill the required number of glasses 3/4 full of sliced pineapple and oranges, and sprinkle a little Kirsch, and Melba sauce mixed together; then cover with vanilla ice cream, and place a small portion of raspberry water-ice on top. Decorate with cherries and whipped cream, and serve quickly.

COUPE LADY EVE

Fill the required number of glasses half full of sliced stewed apples, and cover with a lemon ice; then place on top of this a small portion of pistachio ice cream. Decorate with a cherry in the center, and serve quickly.

PETITS FOURS

sponge cake petit fours (small squares)
2 cups granulated sugar
1/8 teaspoon cream of tartar
1 tablespoon soft butter
1 cup hot water
1 pound powdered sugar

Combine granulated sugar, cream of tartar and water. Cook and stir over medium heat until sugar dissolves. Cook to 226-degrees without stirring. Wash down sugar crystals on sides of pan with a brush dipped in water. Cool to 110-degrees. Blend in confectioners sugar gradually, beating until smooth. Add butter. Thin down frosting with a few teaspoons hot water until pouring consistency. Place petits fours on wire rack over waxed paper. Slowly pour frosting by teaspoon over the cakes. Spread evenly with a small spatula. Serves six.

SPUMONI

3 cups (1 1/2 pints) strawberry ice cream, softened
3 cups (1 1/2 pints) pistachio ice cream, softened
3 cups (1 1/2 pints) chocolate ice cream, softened

Line a loaf pan with waxed paper. Spread strawberry ice cream in an even layer in the bottom of the lined pan; freeze for 30 minutes. Spread pistachio ice cream in an even layer over strawberry; freeze for 30 minutes. Spread chocolate ice cream in an even layer over pistachio; cover with waxed paper and freeze until firm, about 8 hours. Unwrap terrine and invert pan over a serving plate. Remove plastic wrap. To serve, cut terrine into 1-inch-thick slices (dip knife in hot water and wipe dry between each slice). Serves six.

PEACH MELBA

6 slices pound cake
3 cups vanilla ice cream
6 peach halves
1 cup raspberry syrup
2/3 cup chopped roasted almonds

Place a slice of pound cake in the bottom of each of 6 dessert bowls. Top each with a scoop of vanilla ice cream and then a peach half, cut side down, on the ice cream. Pour over some syrup and sprinkle with the almonds. Serves six.

RICE PUDDING

3/4 cup uncooked white rice
2 cups milk, divided
1/3 cup white sugar
1/4 teaspoon salt
1 egg, beaten
2/3 cup golden raisins
1 tablespoon butter
1/2 teaspoon vanilla extract

Bring 1 1/2 cups of water to a boil. Add rice and stir. Reduce heat, cover and simmer for 20 minutes. In another saucepan, combine 1 1/2 cups cooked rice, 1 1/2 cups milk, sugar and salt. Cook over medium heat until thick and creamy, 15 to 20 minutes. Stir in remaining 1/2 cup milk, beaten egg and raisins. Cook 2 minutes more, stirring constantly. Remove from heat, and stir in butter and vanilla. Serve warm. Serves four.

JOAN FONTAINE'S BANANAS WITH RUM

6 bananas
1 tablespoon butter
juice of 1 orange
2 tablespoons lemon juice
1 tablespoon grated orange peel
1 tablespoon grated lemon peel
1/4 cup brown sugar
1/2 cup dark rum

Split the bananas lengthwise, fry in butter, adding first the orange and lemon juice, then the orange and lemon peel and brown sugar. When bananas are tender, light the rum and pour over them. Serves four.

CAFÉ DIABLE

2 ounces Cognac
1 ounces Cointreau
1 ounces White Curacao
6 cups hot coffee
2 cinnamon sticks
8 cloves

Heat ingredients (except coffee) in a pan. When warn, ignite and slowly stir in the coffee until the flames are out. Serves six.

IRISH COFFEE

1 1/2 ounces Irish whiskey
1 teaspoon brown sugar
6 ounces hot coffee
heavy cream

Combine whiskey, sugar and coffee in a mug and stir to dissolve. Float cold cream gently on top. Do not mix.

COCKTAILS

THE STORK CLUB COCKTAIL

1 1/2 ounces top shelf gin
1/2 ounce triple sec
1/4 ounce lime juice
1 ounce orange juice

Stir with ice and strain into a 4-ounce wine glass.

MANHATTAN COCKTAIL

2/3 ounce rye whiskey
1/3 ounce Italian vermouth

Garnish with maraschino cherry, stir, and serve in a 3-ounce cocktail glass.

JOHN GARFIELD'S ROB ROY

2 ounces Scotch
3/4 ounce Italian vermouth
1 dash orange bitters

Garnish with maraschino cherry, stir, and serve in a 3-ounce cocktail glass.

DRY MARTINI

2/3 ounce dry gin
1/3 ounce French vermouth

Stir, garnish with olive and serve in a 3-ounce cocktail glass.

ROSALIND RUSSELL

2/3 jigger aquavit
1/3 jigger Italian vermouth

Shake or stir and serve in the same manner as a Martini.

WILLARD PARKER'S PARKEROO

2 ounces dry sherry
1 ounce tequila
twist of lemon peel

Pour ingredients over shaved ice in a champagne coupe glass.

CLOVER CLUB

1 1/2 ounce gin
4 dashes grenadine
juice of half lemon
1 egg white

Shake over ice and strain into a 4-ounce wine glass.

BRONX COCKTAIL

1 ounce gin
3/4 ounce Italian vermouth
3/4 ounce French vermouth
1/4 ounce orange juice

Shake over ice and strain into a 3-ounce cocktail glass.

NEW YORKER COCKTAIL

2 ounces rye
juice of half lime
1 teaspoon sugar
1 dash grenadine
twist of orange peel

Shake over ice and strain into a 3-ounce cocktail glass.

ALEXANDER

1 1/2 ounce gin
3/4 ounce crème de cacao
1/2 ounce fresh cream

Shake over ice and strain into a 4-ounce cocktail glass.

NELSON EDDY'S ALEXANDER THE GREAT

1/2 ounce crème de cacao
1/2 coffee liqueur
1/2 ounce fresh cream
1 1/2 ounce vodka

Shake over ice and strain into a 4-ounce cocktail glass.

RALPH BELLAMY'S SCOTCH SOUR

3 ounces orange juice
2 ounces lemon juice
6 ounces Scotch whisky
1 teaspoon honey
1 dash Angostura bitters

Mix in a Waring blender and serve frozen with a piece of preserved ginger on a stick.

MARY PICKFORD COCKTAIL

2 ounces rum
3/4 ounce pineapple juice
3 dashes grenadine

Shake over ice and strain into a 3-ounce cocktail glass.

ANN SHERIDAN COCKTAIL

2/3 ounce Bacardi rum
1/3 ounce orange curacao
Juice of half lime

Shake over ice and strain into a 3-ounce cocktail glass.

AVIATION COCKTAIL

2 ounces gin
juice of half lemon
4 dashes maraschino

Shake over ice and strain into a 3-ounce cocktail glass.

SOCIETY COCKTAIL

1 3/4 ounce gin
3/4 ounce French vermouth
4 dashes grenadine

Shake over ice and strain into a 3-ounce cocktail glass.

LUCILLE BALL'S PINK LADY

1 3/4 ounces gin
1/2 ounce applejack
4 dashes grenadine
1 egg white

Shake over ice and strain into a 4-ounce wine glass.

ANNE JEFFREYS' GOLDEN FIZZ

1 1/2 ounces gin
1 egg yolk
1/2 tablespoon sugar
juice of half lemon
soda water

Shake over ice and strain into a highball glass. Fill with soda water and serve.

ARTHUR BERRY'S KICKING COW

1/3 ounce maple syrup
1/3 ounce cream
2/3 ounce bourbon or rye

Shake well with cracked ice and serve in tall glass.

EDDIE WHITTMER'S BLESSED EVENT

2 ounces applejack
2 ounces Benedictine
juice of half lime
dash of curacao

Shake over ice and strain into a cocktail glass.

COOPERSTOWN

1 3/4 ounce gin
1/2 ounce French vermouth
1/2 ounce Italian vermouth
2 sprigs mint

Shake over ice and strain into a 3-ounce cocktail glass.

WARD EIGHT

2 ounces rye
juice of half lemon
4 dashes grenadine

Shake well with cracked ice and serve in tall glass.

FRENCH 75

2 ounces gin
1 teaspoon powdered sugar
juice of half lemon
cracked ice

Top with champagne and serve in tall glass.

CHAMPAGNE COCKTAIL

1 cublet sugar, doused with Angostura bitters
twist of lemon peel

Add cublet of sugar to a wide-brimmed champagne coupe. Fill the glass almost to the top with chilled champagne. Don't stir, but do add a twist of lemon peel.

The Stork Club Cookbook

Lucius Beebe

MORNING AT THE STORK CLUB

It is a matter of common acceptance that even the most firmly established usages are subject to the mutations of time, and that what was yesterday a practice confined to the far side of the railroad tracks (a part of town often frequented by the best people but always in closed hacks) is today definitely au fait in Mayfair. The concern of men of intelligence is not so much with what may be fashionable as with what is reasonable, and, while the notion of drinking cocktails directly after breakfast may seem at first consideration an eminently unchristian practice, this has not always been the case.

Disregarding as impertinent to the important matter in hand all learned controversy over the origin of the word cocktail, whether it sprung from the Aztec Xochitl or from the custom of compounding the arrangement with a chicken's feather for ornamental panache, the cocktail as it is known today first achieved widespread acceptance, so far as diligent research can establish, in the middle years of the nineteenth century.

It gained favorable mention in the fifties and sixties as the midmorning slug of the captains of industry and finance on whose waistcoats it was practicable to play games and who rode downtown from Murray Hill to Wall Street after a breakfast which would founder today's fragile souls who face the day fortified by an eyedropper filled with orange juice and a slice of Melba toast. In the President-Grant-and-Erie-common age drinking was a notably masculine occupation and it went hand in hand with chewing tobacco and owning large stables. Everything was big; the whisky slug was four ounces, the cuspidors in the Astor House might reasonably be confused with umbrella stands, and the business of agitating the liver and stirring the senses into function began early in the day.

Gentlefolk often drank a brandy sling heavily laced with Stoughton's Bitters, a notable cure-all of the times, before descending to breakfast. Hardier if less elegant souls had a slug of rock and rye while shaving and brushed their teeth in a light Moselle. The square hat compartment which was part of every man's chiffonier of the period was often as not devoted, not to father's best gray topper from Yourmans, but to a bottle of Lawrence's Medford Rum, a chummy bedroom companion and an aid in tying the complicated stocks and Ascots then in sartorial favor.

During the ride downtown the pre-breakfast restorative, no matter how liberally applied, tended to die on the captains of finance and industry and a few of the less sensitive of that valiant generation paused at spas previously ascertained and charted near Canal Street before continuing to the shadow of Grace Church, but this was frowned on by the conservative or J. P. Morgan element which maintained that a man should be able to read his own mail, at least the first delivery, unaided by the office staff.

One skirmish with the stock ticker, however, and a whiff of what Jay Gould was doing in the gold market usually set even the Morgan partners to reaching for their hats and telling the'receptionist they were just going across the street to the Subtreasury for a few minutes. They invariably returned from the Subtreasury eating a clove.

This practice, mark you, of midmorning refreshment originally carried with it no least suggestion of relinquished moral control or decline in individual deportment. It was as commonly accepted and respectable a ritual at the period of which we write as is the high noon sour or a restorative milk punch today and had about it no implication of devoting the day to fun or chartering a hack to drive to City Island for lunch. Midmorning was the first well-established masculine cocktail hour.

In an age when stem glassware was less common than it is today cocktails were served in what is now known as a Delmonico glass, a practice still observed at Whyte's and a few other old-time restaurants in the financial district, and ran in quantity to the size of a modern sour. Because of its unrivaled tonic qualities as a restorative and element for firming the moral fiber, as well as because of the prevailing American taste for drinks with whisky bases at this time, the classic and standard Manhattan cocktail, precisely as it is served at this red hot minute at the Stork Club, was an almost universal rite until the end of the nineteenth century.

MANHATTAN COCKTAIL

⅔ oz. rye whisky
⅓ oz. Italian vermouth
Decorate with maraschino cherry, stir, and serve in 3 oz. cocktail glass.

Whatever may be the present vogue for Martinis, a drink which became firmly established as Londons type gin became more widely available in the United States, make no mistake about it: the Manhattan was the archetypal short mixed drink and blazed a trail for all others to follow. Nor, accomplished bartenders will point out, is it necessary or even advisable to use the finest and oldest proof spirits in making the most acceptable Manhattan. The smoother and sweeter the whisky, the less volume or incisiveness will be possessed by the finished cocktail and it has often been remarked that the most exciting Manhattan is one compounded with ordinary quality bar whisky rather than the rarest overproof article. It is perhaps the only mixed drink where this generality obtains.

There are, of course, a good many redactions and variations of the Martini which depends for its sweetness or dryness on the proportions with which gin and vermouth are used, but the standard and universal dry Martini is still the simplest and most effective mixed drink ever devised:

DRY MARTINI

⅔ oz. Londons or dry gin
⅓ oz. French vermouth
Stir, decorate with olive and serve in 3 oz. cocktail glass.

The perfect Martini, somewhat smoother and less potent to the taste, is achieved by using the same proportions of gin and vermouth, but equal parts of French and Italian vermouth are used, in other words 1/6 oz. each in the above formula. The Gibson, long a favorite with discriminating, older drinkers, was first, according to the legend, evolved by the late Charles Dana Gibson at the bar of the Plaza Hotel in New York and was made with a pickled onion for ornament instead of the traditional green olive.

A vast deal of pother has from time to time been raised over the almost fanciful advantages of stirring over shaking Martinis. The almost universal custom is for stirring them, but Marco, head barman at New York's celebrated Colony Restaurant, makes a practice of shaking them vigorously and candor compels the admission that the only discernible difference between the two products is that a spooned Martini is crystal clear while a shaken one inclines to a clouded appearance. Bar practice at the Stork favors the noncontroversial stirring or spooning, but the management will oblige by having them compounded in a cement mixer or butter chum if that is what the customer wants. When drinking Martinis, Cookie, the barkeep, remarks, the customer is almost always right.

Other variations are common and many of them legitimate, such as the alternate devised a number of years ago by Steve Hannagan of using a dry sherry instead of vermouth for a particularly lethal Martini, and a drink thoughtfully named for herself by Rosalind Russell, the secret of which should be guarded like that of the atom bomb, but which she is willing the world shall share if she is held blameless of the results:

ROSALIND RUSSELL

⅔ jigger Danish Alborg aquavit
⅓ jigger vermouth or dubonnet
Shake or spoon and serve in the same manner as a Martini.

Miss Russell's own comment on this arrangement is: "My father-in-law, Carl Brisson, introduced me to this drink and six months later I married his son!"

In a less heroic generation, however, it must be recorded that few demands are received across the bar of the Stork for cocktails until after the sun has crossed the proverbial yardarm at noon. Public taste in restoratives, pick-me-ups and simple, old-fashioned drinking for pleasure runs more to longer and taller drinks and less to the concentrated essence of life to be encountered in cocktails.

As is entirely natural in such a highly individualized occupation, requirements for morning drinks vary with almost every forenoon drinker. There may be a certain or prevailing similarity of tastes at more conventional hours and the steward can count upon a fairly regular dispensation of, say, Martinis at lunchtime or Daiquiris before dinner, but the A.M. elbow bender is a Maverick, a lone wolf and there is no predicting his vagrant whim or fancy.

If his innards require gentling and the virtues of nourishment at the same time, his requirement may be for a milk punch or fizz with eggs. He may demand the moderate advancement of the governing throttle implicit in a sour or simple highball, or he may call in impassioned tones for the alcoholic equivalent of adrenalin and oxygen, the quick emergency functions of Stinger, Scotch Mist or a Sundowner Cocktail.

It is in the early watches that the knowing and perceptive bar- keep must most closely fill the function of physician and adviser. His clients are in humbled or quiescent mood, usually in search of soft words and consolation. By noontime he may be in requisition as adviser on the race track situation and by nightfall, variously in demand as councillor at love, bail bondsman or bouncer, but in the morning his technique is guided by a strictly bedside manner.

Some of the more conventional restoratives during the placid hours when the laundry is delivering the waiter's aprons and the day's beer is cooling in the coils are:

MILK PUNCH (PLAIN)

½ pt. milk
1 tsp. sugar
Shake, strain and serve in 12 oz. glass and put little nutmeg on top.

SHERRY FLIP

2 oz. sherry wine
1 tsp. sugar
whole egg
Shake well. Nutmeg on top. Use wine glass.

PORT FLIP

2 oz. port wine
1 tsp. sugar
whole egg
Shake well. Nutmeg on top. Use wine glass.

SHERRY EGGNOG

1 egg
2 oz. sherry
1 tsp. sugar
milk
Shake, strain and serve in tall glass. Nutmeg on top.

BALTIMORE EGGNOG

1 fresh egg
½ tbsp. fine granulated sugar
¼ jigger brandy
¼ jigger Jamaica rum
½ pt. fresh milk
Shake well and strain into highball glass.
Serve with a grating of nutmeg.

PORT EGGNOG

1 egg
2 oz. port wine
1 tsp. sugar
milk
Shake, strain and serve in tall glass. Nutmeg on top.

If, by reason of ill-advised research among the flagons the night before, scholarship has triumphed over discretion; if in a word the entire human person resembles nothing so much as what the author of this volume's first city editor, Norton Pratt of the Boston *Telegram.* used to define as "a basket of busted bungholes," Burgess Meredith has a cure for it. It's called "London Fog."

LONDON FOG

1½ oz. gin
¼ oz. Pernod's absinthe
Frappe briskly with shaved ice and serve while still foaming

This, of course, is among the more heroic remedies, and a few of the less lethal and drastic cures available to the almost illimitable resources of Cookie are the following:

WHISKY SOUR

2 oz. whisky
Juice of half lemon
1 tsp. sugar
Shake, strain and serve in Delmonico glass.
Dress with fruit. Squirt of seltzer.

BRANDY EGGNOG

1 egg
2 oz. brandy
1 tsp. sugar
milk
Shake, strain and serve in tall glass with nutmeg on top.

EGG SOUR

1 tsp. fine granulated sugar
3 dashes lemon juice
1 oz. curacao
1 oz. brandy
1 egg
Shake with cracked ice and strain into Delmonico glass.

RUM EGGNOG

1 egg
2 oz. rum
1 tsp. sugar
milk
Shake, strain and serve in tall glass with nutmeg on top.

PORT WINE COBBLER

Fill goblet with fine ice
3 oz. port wine

1 tsp. sugar
Stir. Decorate with fruit—sprig of mint.
Straws.

Jean Hersholt's version of a perfect pick-me-up is:

PICK-ME-UP

1 oz. French vermouth
1 oz. cherry brandy
¼ oz. dry gin
Should be served frozen cold in a large cocktail or Delmonico glass and
consumed before it has a chance to warm up.

This last generality contained in Mr. Hersholt's directions for restoring animation to the flagging torso is one which, generally speaking, applies to all short drinks in the cocktail and sour class and to the complicated chemistry of pick-me-ups in particular. Old-time barkeeps had a phrase for it: "Drink it while it's laughing at you." And that is the way these drinks should be downed, immediately and with dispatch, not lovingly sipped like a liqueur or allowed to come to a slow boil in the hand like a bankrupt's highball. It is neither the mark of a pig nor an alcoholic to get these drinks insinuated into the system with a maximum of dexterity because that is the way they were made to be drunk. The cocktail never could have come into existence without ice and, to this day, is notably not in demand in parts of the world where ice is a scarce commodity. For the record shows that the Falernian of Nero and other prominent Romans was served chilled with the snows of the Appenines, but backward communities ever since have resisted the devisings of refrigeration as in England, where the iced highball is frowned on as on a par with the short jacket in the evening, although civilization is reported slowly to be advancing even within the straitened confines of the Tight Little Island.

Among the more exotic of the restorative category is a sort of bastard Martini evolved by Willard Parker with all the ingredients cockeyed as well as the consumer:

PARKEROO

2 oz. dry sherry
1 oz. tequila
twist of lemon peel.
Pour this concoction over shaved ice, allow to chill and then pour into
pre-chilled champagne coup glass.

"While painting a picket fence around my house," deposes Mr. Parker, "I discovered that after two Parkeroos I could remain stationary and let the fence revolve around the brush. This will give you an idea!"

No less effective in the realm of non-academic medicine for morning use may be found the following patent nostrums, some of them dating from grandma's day and all of them esteemed as sovereign remedies:

RUM TODDY

1½ oz. Jamaica rum
1 tsp. sugar
2 cloves
slice of lemon
cinnamon
Serve in old-fashioned glass. Add boiling water or cold water as the case may be.

SHERRY COBBLER

fill goblet with fine ice
3 oz. sherry
1 tsp. sugar
1 twist lemon peel
add dash of cherry brandy
Stir. Decorate with fruit, sprig of mint.

MORNING GLORY FIZZ

1½ oz. Scotch
1 tsp. powdered sugar
white of egg
½ tsp. sugar
Shake and strain in highball glass. Top with seltzer.

BRANDY FLIP

2 oz. brandy
1 tsp. sugar
whole egg
Shake well. Nutmeg on top. Use 4 oz. wine glass.

SOUTH SIDE FIZZ

1½ oz. gin
juice of half lemon
2 sprigs of mint
1 tsp. sugar
Shake well, strain into highball glass and add seltzer. Decorate with mint.

Amidst this scholarly discussion of the uses of advanced medicine in the treat-
ment and cure of you know what, there may well be considered two classic
stand-bys which have engaged the speculative attentions of amateurs for many
years, the prairie oyster and champagne in various solutions. The prairie oyster
is an old-time favorite of such stalwart Irish saloonkeepers as the late, great Dan
Moriarity and can be served either with or without the liquor ingredient. It possesses the advantage of extremely hot content along with the nutritional value of
raw egg which has long been known as one of the most easily digested foodstuffs:

PRAIRIE OYSTER

yolk of egg
1 dash Lea & Perrin's Sauce
red pepper and salt to taste
1½ oz. brandy or madeira
Serve in old-fashioned glass. Dash of vinegar on top.

Champagne in the morning is a variously advantageous drink and is practically
the only wine which lends itself to absorption twenty-four hours around the
clock. About the only standard that can be applied to it is whether or not you are
in the mood for the stuff. There are mornings, especially in spring and summer
when nature herself is in a clement mood and the shakes are not too overpower-
ing, when nothing seems as auspicious as a very cold bottle of Veuve Clicquot,
Mumm's or Charles Heidsick in a very dry cuvée. If the senses are attuned to its
reception this can be a happy-making way to start the day, but the slightest dis-
cord between the wine and the palate may lead to catastrophe.

There is a school of thought, leaders among whose ranks are such notables as
Howard Barnes, the learned drama reporter, Frank Sullivan and the late Berry
Wall, which places its faith in that curious admixture of wine and Guinness's
stout known as Black Velvet. Their claim that it soothes and gentles the recalci-
trant stomach and, all guileful and unperceived, overcomes the jangled nerves is
doubtless well founded. On the other hand, there are those who, confronted with
two or three tall glasses of this potation, lapse into what Milt Gross calls "a dip
slip". Certainly it is a heavy arrangement and may result in the achievement of a
state of benign stupefaction by the unwary.

BLACK VELVET

½ dry champagne
½ Guinness stout
Chill these separately and pour them together in equal portions in any
  available tall glass holding at least a pint.

Less esoteric than either of the foregoing and, perhaps, more suited to the purse
and pretentions of the average victim of breakfast time palsy are some of these,
all of which are accessible and some of them in frequent requisition among the
Stork's eleven o'clock patrons:

ROB ROY

2 oz. Scotch
¾ oz. Italian vermouth
1 dash orange bitters
Decorate with cherry. Stir and serve in 3 oz. cocktail glass.

SCOTCH MIST

1½ oz. Scotch
With shaved ice —serve in old-fashioned glass. Twist of lemon peel. Serve
  with straws.

GIN SMASH

1½ oz. gin
crush half lump sugar with 3 sprigs of mint
1 cube ice
fruit
Serve in old-fashioned glass. Top with seltzer. Stir.

Travelers who have made the grand tour to New Orleans, where the absorption
of nourishment in liquid form, whether on a medicinal basis or in unabashed
search for worldly pleasure and satisfaction, begins at an extremely early hour
and where northerners are sometime surprised, although never dismayed, to
find the natives drinking Martinis at breakfast, will recall the favorite drinks at
such favorite places as the St. Regis, the bar of the St. Charles Hotel, the Old
Absinthe House and the long bar of the Roosevelt. Here, before the noonday
papers are on the streets, the exquisities of America's oldest urban civilization
foregather to contrive ways of losing money on horses and other amiable follies
and to command the long, tall drinks that are the essence of urbane and mannered

conviviality. The late, lamentable Huey Long, short on virtues as he may have been, at least was the ambassador to the world of the Ramos or Remus fizz and this may be his monument to immortality.

RAMOS FIZZ

2 dashes of orange flower water
juice of half lemon
2 oz. gin
1 oz. cream
1 egg white
Shake very well, strain into tall glass and fill with seltzer. Collins glass.

Governor Long once gave a demonstration of the architecture and consumption of various native Louisiana drinks for the benefit of the reporters and other servants of democracy at the bar of the New Yorker Hotel and, though there were those present who might condemn his brand of politics, there was no one who would even implicitly reproach either his virtuosity as a barkeep or his capacity as his own best customer.

Candor compels the admission that to absorb the native beverages of New Orleans it is most advantageous to be in New Orleans itself. Other atmospheres are vaguely hostile to the leisured formality and circumstance required both for the devising and appreciation of flips and fizzes while much of the charm of their consumption derives from the cool of a sequestered courtyard, such as the Court of the Two Sisters, or from a glimpse, over the shoulders of happy customers, of the dazzling pavement of Canal Street outside. The Stork has them on tap, however, and if such added inducements to their appreciation as gumbo filé, pompano en papillot or fat fresh shrimp right from the Louisiana bayous are required, these too are available on the Stork menu.

Generally speaking, fizzes, flips and cocktails depending for part of their consistencies on the presence of egg, egg white or cream seem closely related to one another and their service appropriate to morning rather than to other times of the day and night when the nature of their economy would tend to impair the appetite for food rather than stimulate it.

ROYAL FIZZ

juice of half lemon
1½ oz. gin
1 tsp. sugar
1 egg
Shake well and strain into highball glass and add seltzer.

SILVER FIZZ

juice of half lemon
1 tsp. sugar
1½ oz. gin
white of egg
Shake well and strain into highball glass.
Add seltzer

"NEW ORLEANS" FIZZ

juice of half lime
juice of half lemon
2 dashes orange flower water
1 tsp. sugar
1 oz. sweet cream
2 oz. gin
white of egg
Shake well, serve in Collins or 12 oz. glass and add a very little seltzer.

DIAMOND FIZZ

juice of one lemon
1 tsp. sugar
Serve in highball glass with one ice cube. Fill with champagne.

GIN FIZZ

juice of one lemon
1 tsp. sugar
1½ oz. gin
Shake, strain and serve in highball glass with 1 cube ice. Fill with syphon.

SLOE GIN FIZZ

juice of half lemon
1 tsp. sugar
1½ oz. sloe gin
Shake well, strain into highball glass and add seltzer.

BRANDY FIZZ

juice of one lemon
1 tsp. sugar 1
1½ oz. brandy
Shake, strain and serve in highball glass with one cube of ice. Fill with
*   syphon.*

SEA FIZZ

1½ oz. absinthe
juice of half lemon
1 tsp. sugar
white of egg
Shake well, strain into highball glass and add seltzer.

COFFEE COCKTAIL

¾ oz. brandy
¾ oz. port wine
1 tsp. sugar
yolk of egg
Shake well and serve in wine glass with nutmeg on top.

An improvement, as some may think, on the conventional Alexander cocktail is
the brainstorm child of Nelson Eddy and he calls it "Alexander the Great".

ALEXANDER THE GREAT

½ oz. crème de cacao
½ oz. coffee liqueur
½ oz. fresh cream
1½ oz. vodka
Shake until cold as Siberia. Watch your Steppes, because more than three
*   of these gives the consumer a wolfish appetite.*

The more conventional Alexander is as follows:

ALEXANDER

1½ oz. gin
¾ oz. crème de cacao
½ oz. fresh cream
Shake and serve in 4 oz. wine glass.

WHITE ROSE

1¾ oz. gin
4 dashes maraschino
4 dashes orange juice
4 dashes lemon juice
egg white
Shake and serve in 4 oz. wine glass.

EAGLE COCKTAIL

1½ oz. gin
¾ oz. crème Yvette
juice of half lemon
1 tsp. sugar
white of egg
Shake and serve in 4 oz. wine glass.

WIDOW'S DREAM

1½ oz. benedictine
whole egg
Shake well, serve in Delmonico glass and fill with cream.

CLOVER CLUB

1½ oz. gin
4 dashes grenadine
juice of half lemon
white of egg
Shake and serve in 4 oz. wine glass.

CAFÉ DE PARIS COCKTAIL

1½ oz. gin
¾ oz. anisette
¾ oz. fresh cream
white of egg
Shake and serve in 4 oz. wine glass with nutmeg on top.

ALEXANDER #2

1½ oz. brandy
¾ oz. crème de cacao
½ oz. fresh cream
Shake and serve in 4 oz. wine glass.

RUM FLIP

2 oz. rum
1 tsp. sugar
whole egg
Shake well. Nutmeg on top. Use wine glass.

PLAIN EGGNOG

1 egg
1 tsp. sugar
milk
Shake, strain and serve in tall glass with nutmeg on top.

BLACKBERRY PUNCH

juice of one lemon
1 tsp. fine granulated sugar
2 oz. blackberry liqueur
1 oz. rum
Shake well with cracked ice and strain into goblet idled with shaved ice.
  Dress with fruit and serve with straws.

STRAWBERRY FIZZ

juice of half lemon
4 mashed strawberries
½ tsp. sweet cream
1 jigger dry gin
Shake well with cracked ice and strain into highball glass. Add one ice
  cube and fill with soda water.

The repertory of morning drink possibilities is practically endless and, indeed, bounded only by the human imagining and the human capacity for absorption. Old-timers will remember barkeeps of the last generation who made a practice of uncapping a bottle of beer by their bedside before retiring and drinking it, flat and warm, the next morning, in the belief that, since the beer was by now separated from its gaseous content, it would be in prime condition for reabsorbing any gas that it might encounter and notably the gas of the human stomach.

Before taking leave of the subject and moving into the less necessitous and urgent category of noontime life at the Stork it may be wise to consider the function of absinthe as a restorative, pick-me-up and general cure-all. It has been held in high esteem for this purpose by countless informed and knowing drinkers and, in all probability, has its uses. The great drawback to its use in the experience of the author, at least, has been its tendency to dull the appetite for food and consequently delay and diminish the consumption of solid food which, in the end, is the greatest of all restoratives after a night among the pots.

Absinthe by reason of its chemistry is probably the briskest and most violent of bitters and there are many who are charmed with its poetic qualities, its historic antecedents, literary associations and other intangible aspects, and there are also many who admire its wormwood flavor and opalescent optical charms when used merely as a flavoring for drinks with other bases.

If the amateur of its properties can really take it or leave it and shift either to a less treacherous drink or to food itself after a couple, there is probably no pick-me-up in the world comparable for immediate efficacy to an absinthe frappe.

ABSINTHE FRAPPE

1½ oz. absinthe, green or white
1 white of egg
1 tsp. sugar
Frappe briskly with shaved ice and serve frozen cold in a Delmonico glass.

Sometimes the name of a drink has nothing to do with its content, occasion or potentialities and represents nothing more than the dead hand of tradition or the momentary whim of its originator or popularizer. On other occasions, however, it is indicative of the nature of the consequence of the potation, and such would seem to be the case with several of the absinthe arrangements hereinafter catalogued. Their precise nature may best perhaps be summarized by the opening lines of the "Cocktail Song" which amateurs of scholarly matter will find in its entirety in *The Stag's Hornbook* and other hand volumes of reference:

"The cocktail is a pleasant drink;
It's nice and harmless, I don't think!"

COMMANDO COCKTAIL

½ oz. bourbon
¾ oz. triple sec
2 dashes pernod

juice of half lime
Shake and serve in 3 oz. cocktail glass.

HURRICANE COCKTAIL

1¼ oz. brandy
¾ oz. pernod
¾ oz. vodka
Shake and serve in 3 oz. cocktail glass.

ABSINTHE DRIP

1½ oz. absinthe
*Dissolve one lump of sugar, using the French drip spoon, and fill glass
    with cold water.*

ABSINTHE COCKTAIL

1½ oz. absinthe
1 white of egg
1 tsp. sugar
Shake. Twist of lemon peel on top. Serve in 4 oz. wine glass.

EARTHQUAKE COCKTAIL

1 oz. gin
1 oz. bourbon
¾ oz. absinthe
Shake and serve in 3 oz. cocktail glass.

To append as a coda to this symphony of thunder a less tumultuous assortment of
morning favorites of long standing with moderate tosspots, such traditional long
and short ones as sloe gin rickies, Tom Collinses, Daiquiris and claret lemonade
are all of them at once convivial, restorative and stimulating to the wit and intel-
lect without being conducive to tumult or public commotion.

SLOE GIN RICKEY

1½ oz. sloe gin
*Insert juice of half lime and rind in highball glass. Fill glass with seltzer
    and stir.*

TOM COLLINS

2 cubes ice
juice of one small lemon
1 tsp. sugar
2 oz. gin
Use tall glass. Fill with soda and shake.

DAIQUIRI

2 oz. silver rum
juice of half lime
1 tsp. sugar
Shake well and serve in 3 oz. cocktail glass.

CLARET LEMONADE

juice of one lemon
1 tsp. sugar
cracked ice in tall glass
top with 3 oz. claret wine
fruit
dash of seltzer
Serve with a straw in Collins glass and decorate with fruit.

And on this note of gentility and restraint it may be announced by the management that luncheon is served.

NOON AT THE STORK CLUB

Transition, in any occupation as delicately balanced as that of purveying or consuming things to drink, can never be abrupt and must be achieved by almost imperceptible degrees. For this reason the passage of time from morning through noon and the change in clientele from those impelled by urgency or social inclination to a few quick ones in the morning to the Stork's patrons who begin drifting in on the imponderable margins of lunchtime is never dramatic. The tides that ebb and flow past the plush rope and through the front bar are hardly ever well defined or abruptly demarked with the single exception of theater hour which is, all over New York, a more or less mathematically fixed time of transition when an old order, nightly and on matinee days, gives place to new.

For this reason the subdivision of this Book of the Hours of the Stork into the three dominant periods of the drinking and eating day and night is almost entirely arbitrary, a device to establish a pattern of chronology and editorial order rather than a factual representation of circumstance. To the casual and uninstructed eye there would probably be small visible difference between the patronage of the bar at one in the afternoon and eight in the evening except for the presence of evening attire among the customers. The knowing observer would note, however, an absence of professional and celebrity faces in the middle of the day, when a feminine clientele is notably in possession, and a corresponding rise in the index of masculinity after dark. It would take a real expert or at least an amateur of New York drinking habits to tell the hour of day from the nature of the drinks being passed across the bar by Cookie and his assistants. There are enough Martinis at midnight and a sufficient flow of champagne at midday to addle the wits of the uninitiate.

As has been suggested above, the midday clientele of the Stork is considerably different from that say of such downtown resorts of masculinity as the Recess Club or Whyte's in that the patrons are predominantly feminine and, even in an age when women's tastes in drinks has begun to approximate if not exactly duplicate that of men, the run of orders is more on the elaborate side than is likely to be the case later in the day.

Glamourous and worldly Gloria Swanson, a celebrity unabashed in her tastes and determined on the best, likes to start the day with what, within the memory of the author used to be known on the Continent as "King's Ruin," because it was the traditional favorite of so many of the old, bearded kings of Europe who used to frequent Foyot's, the Cafè de Paris, Maxim's and the Ritz in the days when the going for kings was good. Miss Swanson prefers to call it more elegantly a champagne cocktail even though she commands it served in a tall Tom Collins glass:

CHAMPAGNE COCKTAIL GLORIA SWANSON

1 pint iced champagne, very dry
2 oz. the best cognac
twist of lemon peel
Served in a tall Tom Collins glass with a cube or two of ice.

Other schools of thought like the same drink in modified containers and with a dash of Angostura Bitters and the author has seen it prepared for such exquisite drinkers as the late King of Spain with a teaspoon of strawberry liqueur in place of the sugar and bitters.

CHAMPAGNE COCKTAIL

1 lump sugar, saturated with Angostura bitters
1 cube of ice
twist of lemon peel
Fill with chilled, champagne and serve in champagne glass.

In the same family as the various versions of champagne cocktail is the celebrated French 75, an elixir which, if it did not actually have its origin in the first of the German wars, at least came to the general attention of American drinkers at that time and was immediately enshrined in the pharmacopoeia of alcohol artistry in the United States upon the conclusion of hostilities in 1919.

"FRENCH 75"

2 oz. gin
1 tsp. powdered sugar
juice of half lemon
cracked ice
Top with champagne and serve in tall glass.

Some less exotic but nonetheless popular noontime cocktails follow:

COOPERSTOWN

1¾ oz. gin
½ oz. French vermouth
½ oz. Italian vermouth
2 sprigs mint
Shake, strain well and serve in 3 oz. cocktail glass.

DUBONNET COCKTAIL

1⅓ oz. dubonnet
1⅓ oz. gin
Twist of lemon peel. Stir and serve chilled in 3 oz. cocktail glass.

CLOVER LEAF

1½ oz. gin
4 dashes grenadine
juice of half lemon
white of egg
mint leaves
Shake and serve in 4 oz. wine glass with sprig of mint on top.

BERMUDA COCKTAIL

1¾ oz. gin
¾ oz. peach brandy
2 dashes grenadine
2 dashes orange juice
Shake and serve in 3 oz. cocktail glass.

BACARDI COCKTAIL

2 oz. Bacardi rum
juice of half lime
1 dash grenadine
Shake and serve in 3 oz. cocktail glass.

CUBAN COCKTAIL

1½ oz. brandy
¾ oz. apricot brandy
juice of half lime
Shake well and serve in 3 oz. cocktail glass.

PANAMA COCKTAIL

1¼ oz. brandy
¾ oz. cream
¾ oz. crème de cacao
Shake and serve in 4 oz. cocktail glass.

COTILLION COCKTAIL

1½ oz. bourbon
½ oz. triple sec
½ oz. orange juice
½ oz. lemon juice
1 dash rum
Shake and serve in 3 oz. cocktail glass.

Long ago in the early Scott Fitzgerald era when collegiate youth down for the weekend from New Haven had never heard of a yet-to-be-born Stork Club, they did their hoisting at a variety of places dominated, over the years of the early twenties, by Matt Winkle's at 381 Park Avenue and the celebrated resort of Dan and Mort Moriarity at 216 East Fifty-eighth Street. The lore and legends of the age are available in other and better suited repositories than here, but one of the institutions of a time when Connie Bennett was the pin-up girl of the Plaza Grill on Saturday afternoons and the tea dance was in its finest flower was the practice of pooling the resources of ten or a dozen undergraduates to reserve a single bedroom at the Commodore Hotel. This served to shave, change to dinner attire and park their luggage in for the weekend, and, by a few simple expedients, such as dismantling the bed of its double mattresses and wedging two customers in the bathtub, as many as fifteen were able to spend the night in such an apartment with a maximum of discomfort and minimum of cash outlay.

Sunday noontime was invariably one of remorse, stock taking, bail raising and attempts to quicken the unidentified dead found in a coma beside the laundry hamper and the sole clue to whose identity was a return ticket to New Haven in the pocket of a Brooks dinner jacket. Usually three or four quarts of gin could be raised among the bottle scarred veterans of Saturday night at the Palais Royal, and it was rendered potable by the simple expedient of calling upon room service for an appropriate quantity of orange water ice and mixing the two in whatever vessels lent themselves handily to the purpose. A solid metal wastebasket was generally approved as ideal, and the stimulant resulting was known to a whole generation of scholars as

COMMODORE BEDROOM

1 qt. Gordon's gin
1 qt. orange water ice
*Shake together in a pitcher or other chalice without other ingredient, as
the water ice provides both chilling and mixer for the gin.*

It will be at once perceived that this was a crude and rough-and-ready make-shift for two cocktails which once exercised a considerable hold upon the general imagination, although of recent years they have been supplanted by other favorites.

BRONX COCKTAIL

1 oz. gin
¾ oz. sweet vermouth
¾ oz. French vermouth
¼ oz. orange juice
Shake and serve in 3 oz. cocktail glass.

ORANGE BLOSSOM

2 oz. gin
¾ oz. orange juice
Shake and serve in 3 oz. cocktail glass.

Another miscellaneous clutch of cocktails which Mr. Billingsley's day-shift Ganymedes report as being in current high favor with the carriage trade include:

WHITE LADY

1½ oz. gin
¾ oz. cointreau
juice of half lemon
egg white
Shake and serve in 4 oz. wine glass.

GIN DAISY

juice of half lemon
4 dashes of grenadine
1½ oz. gin
Serve in goblet with fine ice, fruit, squirt of seltzer. Straws.

EL PRESIDENTE COCKTAIL

1½ oz. rum
1¼ oz. French vermouth
2 dashes grenadine
twist of orange peel
Shake and serve in 3 oz. cocktail glass.

Should the matter of food, at an appropriate pause in the rounds of restoratives, rear its dainty head at this juncture, the management of the Stork stands ready and willing to purvey certain dishes which have become favorites with luncheon patrons and half a dozen of which are here briefly mentioned. All standard variations on the luncheon theme may be taken for granted as available on the ample house menu; these are specialties and indigenous to the premises at No. 3 East Fifty-third Street.

Omelette Steve Hannagan was named for one of the Stork's first patrons, oldest inhabitants and the closest confident of the management for no more elusive reason than that Mr. Hannagan favors his omelette garnished with diced mushrooms, fried eggplant and stewed tomatoes.

Shirred Eggs Bibesco are compounded with a julienne of tongue, mushrooms and the best Perigordine truffles in a Madeira sauce, while Scrambled Eggs Divette are lovingly chafed in fresh butter and thick cream and garnished with sliced Louisiana shrimps of outsize proportions in a shrimp sauce with asparagus tips.

If something more robust is in order, there is Minced Chicken Montlord: whole slices of thick white meat in cream sauce, illustrated with truffles and mushrooms and interlaced with Virginia ham in long slices.

Calves Liver Hommil is a familiar saute of liver with the added feature supplied by sauce Smitaine, while Veal Sweetbreads Rose Marie are broiled with half tomato, French fried eggplant, the heads of fresh mushrooms and Madeira sauce.

The tally of noontime drinks which pass as currency over the square mahogany in the Stork front room are as various as the personalities of the "name" patrons who command them, running from the simple double Scotch and soda which is invariable with Edward Arnold, the brandy and cognac highball described elsewhere but known to George Sanders as "Saint's Halo," and the double glass of California claret affected by Nigel Bruce to the secret concoction made for her friends by Dame May Whitty and called "Dame's Downfall," which not even Cookie by counting the bottles called for has been able to analyze, and Brock Pemberton's simple and Spartan preference, "grape or apple."

Other "over the yardarm" calls, the record attests, frequently come for:

JACK ROSES

2 oz. applejack
juice of half lemon

4 dashes grenadine
Shake and serve in 3 oz. cocktail glass.

GIN SLING

1½ oz. gin
sugar to taste
Serve in 8 oz. highball glass with 2 cubes of ice. Fill with carbonic. Twist of lemon peel.

WHISKY DAISY

juice of half lemon
4 dashes of grenadine
1½ oz. whisky
Serve in goblet with fine ice, fruit, squirt of seltzer.

JOHN COLLINS

use tall glass
2 cubes ice
juice of one small lemon
1 tsp. of sugar
2 oz. Holland gin
Fill with soda and stir.

APPLEJACK SOUR

2 oz. applejack
juice of half lemon
1 tsp. sugar
Shake, strain and serve in Delmonico glass.
Dress with fruit. Squirt of seltzer.

SEPTEMBER MORN COCKTAIL

2 oz. Bacardi rum
juice of half lime
4 dashes grenadine
Add egg white. Shake and serve in 4 oz. wine glass.

STAR DAISY

juice of half lemon
4 dashes grenadine
1½ oz. applejack
Serve in goblet with fine ice, fruit, squirt of seltzer.

RUM DAISY

juice of half lemon
4 dashes of grenadine
1½ oz. rum
Serve in goblet of fine ice. Fruit and squirt of seltzer.

DOCTOR COCKTAIL

1½ oz. Swedish punch
juice of half lime
¾ oz. Jamaica rum
Shake and serve in 3 oz. cocktail glass.

AMER-PICON HIGHBALL

2 oz. Amer-Picon
¾ oz. grenadine or lemon syrup
1 cube ice
Serve in highball glass. Fill with syphon. Stir.

DEPTH BOMB

1½ oz. apple brandy
1 oz. brandy
4 dashes grenadine
4 dashes lemon juice
Shake and serve in 4 oz. wine glass.

Generally speaking, the history of the origins and evolution of a particular drink are lost in the shades of antiquity or of last evening as the case may be. Not so the Ward Eight. Perhaps because it came into being in a community noted for the orderliness of its thoughts and its fastidious devotion to history, perhaps because of the circumstance that it first saw the light of day in premises particularly favored by newspaper men and other literati, we know where and approximately when the Ward Eight first leaped at the throat of an astonished world.

Locke-Ober's Winter Place Wine Rooms, a venerable Boston institution and still to this day the town's foremost restaurant, tap- room and resort of masculinity, was located in the eighties as it is today in Winter Place, a short news running between Temple Place and Winter Street or, if you prefer, between the Five Cent Savings Bank and Stowell the jeweler. But a stone's throw from the Massachusetts State House on Beacon Hill and famed for its lobster Savannah and planked steaks, it was natural that Locke's should be a resort of politicians and followers of the political scene. Locke's was not and is not in Boston's Ward Eight, but in the period under consideration Ward Eight was a dominant political subdivision of the community and it was natural that a new drink should be christened for this powerful arrondissement. Although the fame of the Ward Eight was carried afar, it remained and is to this day a particular favorite in Boston and, if the thirsty enquirer is in the vicinity of Brimstone Corner, he can conveniently drop by Locke's, admire the oldest cash register in North America, the Tom and Jerry machine, the splendid barroom nude, and have a Ward Eight in the scene of its origin and first fame.

WARD EIGHT

2 oz. rye
juice of half lemon
4 dashes grenadine
Shake and serve in tall glass with cracked ice, fruit.

As a geographic alternative to this Old Colony highball there is always available:

NEW YORKER COCKTAIL

2 oz. rye
juice of half lime
1 tsp. sugar
1 dash grenadine
twist of orange peel
Shake and serve in 3 oz. cocktail glass.

For no visible regional reason or logic, it was a New Orleans drink which for many years and when built around a substantial base of one of the bourbons listed by S. S. Pierce, the Boston grocers, was a ranking favorite on the New Haven's crack five o'clock, the Merchant's Limited, on the New York-Boston run.

SAZARAC

1 dash pernod in old-fashioned glass
1 lump sugar saturated with Peychaud bitters
1 cube ice
twist of lemon peel
twist of orange peel
1½ oz. bourbon
Stir.

MAMIE TAYLOR

2 cubes ice in tall glass
2 oz. Scotch
slice lemon
1 split ginger ale
Stir.

GIN AND TONIC

2 oz. gin
2 cubes of ice
slice of lemon
Serve in tall glass. Fill with tonic water and stir.

NATIONAL COCKTAIL

2 oz. rum
2 dashes apricot brandy
½ oz. pineapple juice
3 dashes lime juice
Shake and serve in 3 oz. cocktail glass.

Students of local habits and customs may, at somewhat greater length than is here practicable, enquire into the reasons for the ever-rising curve in the chart of the pale cocktail rums and sugar brandies which during the past twenty years have emerged so largely on the American imagination. One reason, obviously, has been the tremendous advertising and promotion campaigns launched by the first and still the dominant manufacturer of sugar brandies, the Cuban firm of Bacardi. Another has been their price which, generally speaking, has been under those of other comparable spirits. A third may well be the feminine factor in public drinking, since it is universally acknowledged that the thin consistency combined with the special suitability of Cuban type rums for mixing with fruits and sugar have a strong appeal to women's taste.

A more oblique angle may be the shrewd approach which was made by the manufacturers and distributors of pale rums through the agency of snob appeal and name publicization. With a knowing eye, Cuban rums, after they had been "discovered" by wealthy travelers and tourists, were first launched in New York and other centers of style, sophistication and manners. The first Cuba Libre the author ever encountered was being drunk by George Jean Nathan in the super-elegant purlieus of the Colony Restaurant and it was from such beginnings as this that the Frozen Daiquiri became as familiar a household property in Social Circle, Georgia, and Fort Madison, Iowa, as the Hoover vacuum cleaner.

The Stork will compound as many drinks with Cuban rums as there are days in the year, but the three which are as dominant in their field as Martinis or Scotch and soda in theirs are:

FROZEN DAIQUIRI

2 oz. silver rum
juice of half lime
1 tsp. sugar
dash of maraschino
shaved ice
Use electric mixer. Serve unstrained in champagne glass with short straws.

CUBA LIBRE

2 oz. rum
insert juice of half lime and rind in tall glass
2 cubes ice
Fill with Coca-Cola
Stir.

"MACARTHUR" COCKTAIL

1½ oz. Bacardi rum
3 dashes Jamaica rum
¾ oz. triple sec or Cointreau
1 dash egg white
Shake and serve in 4 oz. wine glass.

Allied to by the common ancestry of the cane but as various in their generations as the names under which they are sold are the more traditional molasses rums which, generally speaking, are higher in flavor and alcoholic content than Cuban rums, darker in color, more pungent of aroma and more sanctioned by long usage as a world commodity. Even to attempt a catalogue of their types would be a Herculean labor, but a few of the more common varieties are Jamaica, Haitian, Demerara, Barbados, Antigua, Virgin Islands, San Domingan, New England, Canadian, Charleston and St. Pierre.

The enormous versatility of molasses rums and the endless changes that can be rung on their combination with other flavors, spirits and bases, have made their use popular over the centuries with all classes of drinkers so that the generic term rum has become synonymous with the word liquor. Rum, perhaps, most commonly suggests punch, but it is, to many an expert and knowing palate, the most distinguished of all bases for refreshment in cocktail form.

OLYMPIA COCKTAIL

1½ oz. rum (Virgin Islands type)
1 oz. cherry brandy
juice of half lime
Shake and serve in 3 oz. cocktail glass.

HONEY BEE

2 oz. Jamaica rum
¼ oz. honey
½ oz. lemon juice
Shake and serve in 3 oz. cocktail glass.

JAMAICA RUM COCKTAIL

2 oz. Jamaica rum
juice of half lime
1 tsp. sugar
Shake and serve in 3 oz. cocktail glass.

SANTA CRUZ DAISY

juice of half lime
2 oz. rum (Santa Cruz type)
3 dashes simple syrup
3 dashes Maraschino
Serve in goblet with finely shaved ice. Garnish with fruit and top with a squirt of soda water.

RUM SLING

1½ oz. Jamaica rum
2 dashes Angostura bitters
Serve in highball glass with cracked ice.
Fill with carbonic. Twist of lemon peel.
Stir.

PLANTER'S PUNCH

⅓ oz. lemon juice
¾ oz. orange juice
4 dashes Curaçao
2 oz. Jamaica rum
Shake and strain into tall glass filled with shaved içe. Decorate with fruit
   and serve with straws.

MOJITO HIGHBALL

2 oz. rum
1 tsp. sugar
juice of half lime and rind
1 cube ice
Serve in highball glass. Fill with soda. Decorate with 3 sprigs of rind. Stir.

If none of the foregoing compounds can abate the grief of a stormy morning,
Cookie may prescribe for the drooping customer a very special pick-me-up
dreamed up in a bemused moment by Ralph Bellamy and known as

"THE BELLAMY SCOTCH SOUR"

3 oz. orange juice
2 oz. lemon juice
6 oz. Scotch whisky
1 tsp. honey
1 dash Angostura bitters
Frappe until frozen cold in a Waring mixer and serve with a piece of
   preserved ginger on a stick. This, says Mr. Bellamy in a triumph of
   understatement, is a drink for lazy Sunday afternoons and requires no
   super selling.

If no such powerful reviver-from-the-dead is required you might try some of these:

REMSEN COOLER

2 oz. gin
1 cube ice
peel rind of lemon in spiral form
1 split soda
Serve in tall glass and stir.

AMERICAN BEAUTY

3 dashes white crème de menthe
½ oz. orange juice
½ oz. grenadine syrup
½ oz. French vermouth
½ oz. brandy
Shake, top with port wine and serve in 4 oz. wine glass.

SUNDOWNER

1½ oz. brandy
¾ oz. Van Der Hum Liqueur
4 dashes lemon juice
4 dashes orange juice
Shake and serve in 3 oz. cocktail glass.

ADMIRAL COCKTAIL

1½ oz. gin
1 oz. cherry cordial
juice of half lime
Shake and serve in 3 oz. cocktail glass.

BETWEEN-THE-SHEETS

¾ oz. rum
¾ oz. brandy

¾ oz. cointreau
juice of half lemon
Shake and serve in 4 oz. wine glass.

LONE TREE COCKTAIL

2 oz. gin
¾ oz. Italian vermouth
Squeeze orange peel on top, stir and serve in 3 oz. cocktail glass.

GIMLET COCKTAIL

1⅓ oz. gin
1⅓ oz. orange juice
Shake with shaved ice and serve in 3 oz. cocktail glass.

BAHAMAS HIGHBALL

2 oz. gin
1 oz. French vermouth
1 slice lemon
tonic water
Serve in highball glass. Stir.

B.V.D. COCKTAIL

1¾ oz. applejack
1 oz. Italian vermouth
Use old-fashioned glass. Stir.

APRICOT COCKTAIL

1½ oz. apricot brandy
1 oz. gin
2 dashes lemon juice
2 dashes orange juice
Shake and serve in 3 oz. cocktail glass.

SANTA ANITA

1½ oz. Scotch
Shake with cracked ice and serve in old- fashioned glass. Twist of lemon peel.

MANUEL QUEZON COCKTAIL

1½ oz. apple and honey
¾ oz. triple sec
juice of half lime
Shake and serve in 3 oz. cocktail glass

If, by the time this point is reached in the Stork's catalogue of vinous and spirituous offerings, either the reader or the bar patron is inclined, in the interest of complete equilibrium, to command solid food, the chef's suggestion for the day may variously embrace:

BLUEFISH SAUTE SHERMAN OR STORK CLUB

Bluefish saute with plain spinach, sliced mushrooms and Meuniére Sauce.

VEAL CHOP SAUTE CONCORDE

Veal chop saute in butter. Garnished with carrots Vichy, mashed potatoes, new peas, Madeira Sauce.

BABY LAMB BOULANGERE

Roast Baby Lamb. Garnished with glaced small onions and salted pork and potatoes Rissole. Mint Sauce.

NOISETTE OF LAMB LAVALLIERE

Noisette of Lamb in butter garnished with julienne of mushrooms and truffles. Puree of celery, Madeira Sauce.

VEAL CUTLET GISMONDA

Breaded Veal Cutlet with half bread crumbs and half grated Parmisan cheese, saute in butter, garnished with plain spinach, sliced mushrooms. Madeira Sauce.

LAMB KIDNEY SAUTE CABARET

Lamb Kidney Saute, Red Wine Sauce. Garnished with small onions, mushrooms, and salted pork.

On the other hand the resources of the bar staff, based on the tastes of customers at the mahogany and the imaginations of generations of serious-minded drinkers, are by no means exhausted by the brief foregoing summaries, which are intended more in the nature of a précis than any definitive handbook. At the risk of making this copy read like the "also among those present" paragraph at the end of a newspaper society item, among those still available, and in demand as afternoon sets in are:

SHAMROCK COCKTAIL

1½ oz. Irish whisky
1 oz. French vermouth
3 dashes green crème de menthe
3 dashes green Chartreuse
Stir and serve in 3 oz. cocktail glass.

CASINO COCKTAIL

2 oz. gin
4 dashes maraschino
4 dashes orange juice
4 dashes lemon juice
Shake and serve in 3 oz. cocktail glass.

ALLIES COCKTAIL

1 ¾ oz. gin
1 oz. French vermouth
dash Kümmel
Serve in 3 oz. cocktail glass.

FLYING FORTRESS

1 oz. brandy
¾ oz. vodka
½ oz. absinthe
½ oz. triple sec
Shake and serve in 4 oz. wine glass.

BAMBOO COCKTAIL

2 oz. dry sherry
¾ oz. Italian vermouth
Stir and serve in 3 oz. cocktail glass.

BOOMERANG

1 oz. rye
¾ oz. French vermouth
¾ oz. Swedish Punch
2 dashes lemon juice
1 dash Angostura bitters
Serve in 4 oz. wine glass.

ANGEL'S KISS

⅔ oz. crème de cacao
⅓ oz. sweet cream on top
Use cordial glass.

BLACKOUT

1¾ oz. gin
¾ oz. blackberry brandy
juice of half lime
Shake and serve in 3 oz. cocktail glass.

DEVIL COCKTAIL

1⅓ oz. brandy
1⅓ oz. green crème de menthe
Shake and serve in 3 oz. cocktail glass.

WHIST COCKTAIL

1½ oz. rum
½ oz. applejack
¾ oz. Italian vermouth
Shake and serve in 3 oz. cocktail glass.

NIGHT AT THE STORK CLUB

It is a cliche of monstrous proportions to remark that day begins at dusk for the Stork Club, but such is indeed the case, and the daylight skirmishes with pots and pans which have been instigated by casual customers have been, in actual fact, a mere rehearsal for the tumult and industry which sets in after six in the evening. Although the Stork is, from the actual record, something less of a night club than it is of a restaurant and less of either than it is a rendezvous of celebrities who may incidentally care to drink, eat and dance, its fame has been founded as a night club and as a night club it has flourished mightily in the public imagination.

The circumstance that there has never been a floor show, the identifying hallmark of any night club ever before heard of, simply doesn't abate the Stork's confusing reputation as a cabaret. More than a hundred patrons or shoppers after amusement enquire, on an average evening, when the floor show starts and are graveled to find there is none, but it is impossible to disabuse suburbia of the notion that the dancing girls will soon come on, and Mr. Billingsley's vicars merely go on denying it year in and year out. In a way, Mr. Billingsley himself is responsible for the legend since, from time to time, he has inaugurated miniature balloon ascensions from which thousand dollar bills have been showered upon the customers, and these and other follies of a similar Tiffanyesque nature have done nothing to discourage the widespread notion that all hell is constantly on tap at No. 3 East Fifty-third Street. There is always an optimistic fringe of customers who persist in the delusion that promptly at midnight Ted Husing, in a gold lame tailcoat, will shoot Bill Corum right in the lobby and that after that a chorus of unearthly Powers models will distribute platinum cigarette cases to the gentlemen present and platina fox stoles to the ladies.

Meanwhile the accustomed and initiate patrons go about their business of gulping and guzzling the best food and drink ever served in any New York night club since Lillian Russell was a tot, and what they gulp and guzzle is the concern of this particular and scholarly thesis.

As has been suggested elsewhere, human determination and free will being what they are, there is no regulating what drinks will suit the taste of whom at what hour, and the best that can be done is to marshal the resources of Cookie's bar in something that may be a reasonable simulacrum of sound taste and probable demand. Scores of patrons of the Stork, after all, command nothing stronger than Poland water or lemon squash, but they are not the proper concern of the moment.

The approach of the dinner hour, which in New York varies between seven o'clock and midnight, is the signal for unloosing Niagaras of Scotch and soda and cloudbursts of Martinis and old- fashioneds. And if you object to the fruit salad, festoons of maraschino cherries, flotsam and jetsam of orange rind and canopies of Japanese parasols and American flags which are served with old-fashioned cocktails in many places, it is possible to obviate all this nuisance value by simply asking for a bourbon toddy. At Jack Bleeck's Artists and Writers saloon hard by the Herald Tribune and in such Hollywood outposts as Mike Romanoffs and Dave Chasen's, it is known for no discoverable reason as a "gag", but its common term is bourbon toddy and by such it goes elsewhere in the land.

BOURBON TODDY

1 lump of sugar saturated with Angostura bitters
twist of lemon
2 oz. bourbon whisky
1 oz. water
2 cubes ice
The sugar should be ground to syrup in the water with a muddler and the whisky and ice added after that.

In its origin and, to the minds of gastronomic purists, the cocktail was originally intended as a brief drink, a quick aperitif to stimulate appetite and stiffen the flagging gustatory senses, but it has passed into accustomed usage as a drink to be absorbed in considerable quantity despite the admonitions of the judicious. A few from the Stork Club's almost illimitable bar book follow at random:

PARISIAN COCKTAIL

1½ oz. gin
1 oz. French vermouth
3 dashes crème de cassis
Shake and serve in 3 oz. cocktail glass.

MARY PICKFORD COCKTAIL

2 oz. rum
¾ oz. pineapple juice
3 dashes grenadine
Shake and serve in 3 oz. cocktail glass.

ROSE COCKTAIL

2 oz. French vermouth
½ oz. Kirsch
¼ oz. grenadine
Stir well and serve in 3 oz. cocktail glass.

MILLIONAIRE COCKTAIL

1¾ oz. sloe gin
½ oz. apricot brandy
½ oz. Jamaica rum

1 dash grenadine
Shake and serve in 4 oz. wine glass.

BOMBAY COCKTAIL

1¼ oz. brandy
¾ oz. Italian vermouth
¾ oz. French vermouth
2 dashes curaçao
Shake and serve in 3 oz. cocktail glass.

RUBY COCKTAIL

2 oz. gin
3 dashes grenadine
¾ oz. applejack
Shake and serve in 3 oz. cocktail glass.

PRESIDENTE COCKTAIL

1⅓ oz. rum
1⅓ oz. Italian vermouth
twist of orange peel
Shake and serve in 3 oz. cocktail glass.

MIAMI COCKTAIL

2 oz. rum
¾ oz. cointreau
4 dashes lemon juice
Shake and serve in 3 oz. cocktail glass.

It has been remarked elsewhere and may profitably be repeated that the food at the Stork is such as frequently engages the interest of diners who are in no way concerned for the celebrities present and wouldn't know Ann Sheridan if they saw her. Long ago as a practical protest against the school of anesthetized gastronomy which insisted that nothing but scrambled eggs and bacon should be included on a night club menu, Mr. Billingsley went all out for the pleasure and satisfaction of those of his guests whose idea of dinner or supper was something beside salami on rye. At one time the Billingsley support of transcendental gastronomy included the maintenance of a daily airplane service between Florida and New York for the ferrying to the Stork of live stone crabs, fresh Gulf pompano and other rare and costly viands from tropic waters. It was Mr. Billingsley who, to the rage and consternation of competitors in the restaurant business, inaugurated the presence at each table of monstrous mounds of gigantic ripe olives and sheaves of fresh Boston Market celery.

The menu has bristled from year to year with game birds from the grouse moors of Scotland, pheasant en plumage, firkins of pâté de foie and casks of Caspian caviar. The waiters tottered under chateaubriands of outsize proportions culled from prize-winning beeves, and the eyes of patrons lovingly caressed menus awash with soups, sorbets and souffles reminiscent of Foyot's in the great days and of Claridge's in London during the spring seasons before the wars.

Three fish dishes which are the pride of the Stork's chef are Mousse of Sole Washington, Broiled Pompano Tyrolienne and Baked Lobster Excelsior. Mousse of Sole, which was first successfully evolved by the great Escoffier at the Savoy in London and has been universally hailed by gourmets as one of the triumphs of modern culinary art because of the difficulty of retaining in concentrated form the flavor of so delicate a fish, is at the Stork poached and garnished with Lobster a l'Americaine and ornamented with diced mushrooms and truffles.

The pompano is broiled and ornamented with a sauce of French onions and stewed tomatoes, while the lobster is a conventional half shell baked with mushroom sauce in the bottom of the shell, a filling of chopped lobster, fresh butter and celery knob and covered and glacéd with American sauce.

A further assortment of bar compounds which the Stork stands ready at a moment's notice to compound before the happy customer begins wading around in the fish course includes:

CZARINA

1 oz. vodka
¾ oz. apricot brandy
½ oz. French vermouth
½ oz. Italian vermouth
Shake and serve in 3 oz. cocktail glass.

AVIATION COCKTAILS

2 oz. gin
juice of half lemon
4 dashes maraschino
Shake and serve in 3 oz. cocktail glass.

DIPLOMAT COCKTAIL

1¾ oz. French vermouth
1 oz. Italian vermouth
dash maraschino
Stir and serve in 3 oz. cocktail glass.

TOVARICH

1½ oz. vodka
1 oz. Kümmel
juice of half lime
Shake and serve in 3 oz. cocktail glass.

DUPLEX

1⅓ oz. French vermouth
1⅓ oz. Italian vermouth
dash Angostura bitters
Stir and serve in 3 oz. cocktail glass.

AMERICAN FLAG CORDIAL

⅓ oz. grenadine
⅓ oz. maraschino
⅓ oz. crème Yvette
Pour very carefully. Use cordial glass.

ROYAL SMILE

1¾ oz. gin
¾ oz. applejack
4 dashes grenadine
juice of half lime
Shake and serve in 3 oz. cocktail glass.

SOUTHERN COMFORT COCKTAIL

1¾ oz. Southern Comfort
juice of half lime

¾ oz. orange liqueur
Shake and serve in 3 oz. cocktail glass.

PARADISE COCKTAIL

1¼ oz. gin
¾ oz. apricot brandy
¾ oz. orange juice
Shake and serve in 3 oz. cocktail glass.

GREENBRIER COCKTAIL

1⅓ oz. gin
1⅓ oz. Italian vermouth
2 sprigs mint
Shake well, strain and serve in 3 oz. cocktail glass.

The Sidecar was, to the best of the knowledge and belief of the author, invented by Frank, steward and senior barkeep of the celebrated Paris Ritz Bar during the golden age of the early twenties.

In an era when Joe Zelli's, Harry's New York Bar and the men's bar on the Cambon side of the Ritz were probably the three best known tippling Taj Mahals in the world and when every Atlantic liner set down hundreds of solvent and thirsty Yanks full of devaluated francs, Frank of the Ritz Bar was a sort of universally recognized king of saloonkeepers and was, in fact, a very pleasant, generous and understanding friend to thousands of Americans. There was nothing either cheap or popular about the Ritz and there was no dandruff on the morning jackets of its customers, who included Evander Berry Wall, the then King of Spain, the Prince of Wales, Phil Plant, William B. Leeds and the Russian Grand Dukes then living in exile in Paris. The men's bar was also the happy romping and stomping ground, in summer, of most of Harvard, Yale and Princeton with an occasional democratic leaven of Williams or Dartmouth.

The Sidecar was invented by Frank, so far as fallible human memory can determine, about 1923 as a sort of companion piece to the Stinger only with even more expensive ingredients. It was always built by Frank for favored customers with the Ritz's own bottling of a Vintage 1865 Cognac and set one back, in this redaction, the then equivalent of five American dollars.

SIDECAR

1¾ oz. brandy
¾ oz. cointreau

juice of half lime
Shake and serve in 3 oz. cocktail glass.

The Stinger, while enjoying a far more universal and less period- design vogue then the Sidecar, is probably the only drink which while properly a cocktail is also an after-dinner liqueur at the same time. Like the Sidecar it can be fashioned as a rich man's drink by the simple expedient of using fine vintage Cognac or as a more modest arrangement by the infusion in its economy of a California brandy. Except to the very exacting and financial taste, an entirely acceptable Stinger can be made if thoroughly chilled with Christian Brothers brandy.

STINGER

1⅓ oz. brandy
1⅓ oz. white crème de menthe
Shake and serve in 3 oz. cocktail glass.

Ray Bolger is fond of a particular version of Scotch and soda to which he refers as a Bolger Over or Spooner Splash which requires the following ingredients:

BOLGER OVER

2 oz. Scotch whisky
2 oz. club soda
1 inch Jack Spooner's thumb

The virtue of the drink, which must be served by Jack Spooner in person, lies in the flavor derived from his thumb in the glass, giving it a peculiar piquancy not available anywhere else.
From the Stork's own bar book come:

DERBY COCKTAIL

2 oz. gin
¾ oz. peach brandy
2 sprigs mint
Shake well and serve in 3 oz. cocktail glass.

HABANEROS

2 oz. Mexican rum
juice of half lime
4 dashes grenadine
Shake and serve in 3 oz. cocktail glass.

BERMUDA ROSE

2 oz. gin
¾ oz. apricot brandy
2 dashes grenadine
Shake and serve in 3 oz. cocktail glass.

FLORIDA COCKTAIL

2 oz. rum
2 dashes green crème de menthe
juice of half lime
½ oz. pineapple juice
sugar to taste
Shake, decorate with 2 sprigs of mint and serve in Delmonico glass.

SANTIAGO COCKTAIL

1¾ oz. rum
¾ oz. triple sec
1 tsp. sugar
juice of half lime
Shake and serve in 3 oz. cocktail glass.

ARMY COCKTAIL

1½ oz. gin
1 oz. sweet vermouth
2 dashes grenadine
slice of orange peel
Shake and serve in 3 oz. cocktail glass.

BALLET RUSSE COCKTAIL

2oz. vodka
½ oz. crème de cassis
4 dashes lime juice
Shake and serve in 3 oz. cocktail glass.

BIJOU

1¼ oz. gin
¾ oz. Chartreuse
¾ oz. Italian vermouth
Decorate with cherry. Twist of lemon peel over drink. Stir and serve in 3
   oz. cocktail glass.

Although of comparatively recent origin and evolution, the Zombie is a drink the precise source of which, like its exact economy, is subject to controversy. The author first encountered it as an aid to practical alcoholism in the celebrated premises of Trader Vic in Oakland, California, and almost immediately after that in a bamboo bar frequented by Hollywood script writers in search of inspiration to more than customary intellectual chaos. It may very well, as advertised, have been imported from far island places or it may just as plausibly have been the fevered brain child of Trader Vic himself, an opportunist whose ethics are unmuffled by any consideration of human well-being, but, whenever it came, the Zombie exploded into fullest flower at the New York World's Fair. It was the principal stock in trade of the Hurricane Bar in Flushing Meadows and was retailed one to a customer at a dollar a sample by a management at once thrifty and mindful of municipal ordinances. Actually it was not as lethal as advertised, but expediency will limit its consumption by the inexperienced, as the variety and proofs of the rums involved are both chancy elements in the human reckoning.

As will be apparent from the complexity of its ingredients, a Zombie is subject to multiple variations. This is the way Cookie can be persuaded to compound them for patrons with the most reassuring references:

ZOMBIAN

1 oz. amber rum
1 oz. silver rum
1 oz. Jamaica rum
4 dashes cherry brandy
4 dashes apricot brandy
1 dash papaya juice
juice of half lime
Serve in tall glass with cracked ice. Top with ½ oz. 151 proof rum. Stir.
   Decorate with green and red cherry and slice of orange. Serve with
   straws.

Nobody seems ever with any impressive degree of persuasiveness to have been able to say just when such arrangements as a Zombie should be served (if ever) and present any logical reason why one time of day or night is any better (or worse) suited to their inhalation. True purists will scream that all mixed drinks save, perhaps, a vermouth cassis or gin and bitters are an abomination, and as such we have no concern with their cant. The fact stands that many people like many drinks at many times; some even going on record to the effect that they like all drinks at any time. The author of this book makes no attempt, save along the broadest of conceivable lines, to indicate the propriety of any given drink at any given time. The only person fit to be an arbiter in such matters is the consumer himself who will, in any case, drink just as he pleases in complete and magnificent disregard for what any authority in the matter may say. Anyhow, the author's Uncle Ned, who early in life absented himself from Framingham, Massachusetts, to live in Paris where he wore for many decades the same pearl gray derby and made astonishing sums of money playing roulette at the Banker's Club, believed the best time to drink an Haute Sauterne was at breakfast. The admission of this family solecism has always seemed an adequate excuse for the exemption of the author from jury duty in any matter of either gastronomic or sartorial taste.

Another clutch of restorative beverages, the individual items of which are more or less common currency just the other side of the red plush cord in Fifty-third Street are:

SOCIETY COCKTAIL

1¾ oz. gin
¾ oz. French vermouth
4 dashes grenadine
Shake and serve in 3 oz. cocktail glass.

APPLEJACK COCKTAIL

1½ oz. applejack
4 dashes grenadine
juice of half lemon
Shake and serve in 3 oz. glass.

FRISCO COCKTAIL

2 oz. bourbon
¾ oz. benedictine
twist of lemon peel
Stir and serve in 3 oz. cocktail glass.

LOCH LOMOND

2 oz. Scotch
2 dashes Angostura bitters
1 dash simple syrup
Shake with shaved ice and serve in 3 oz. cocktail glass.

SCOTCH RICKEY

1½ oz. Scotch
insert juice of half lime and rind in highball glass
1 cube ice
Fill glass with seltzer and stir.

SCOTCH "COOLER"

2 oz. Scotch
1 cube ice
peel rind of lemon in spiral form
1 split soda
Serve in tall glass and stir.

RED LION

1½ oz. gin
¾ oz. grand marnier
3 dashes grenadine
¼ oz. lemon juice
Shake and serve in 3 oz. cocktail glass.

GIN BUCKS

2 oz. gin
juice of half lemon
2 cubes of ice
Serve in tall glass, fill with ginger ale and stir.

PINK LADY

1¾ oz. gin
½ oz. applejack

4 dashes grenadine
egg white
Shake and serve in 4 oz. wine glass.

STAR COCKTAIL

1¾ oz. applejack
1 oz. Italian vermouth
Stir and serve in 3 oz. cocktail glass.

RUSSIAN COCKTAIL

1 oz. gin
1 oz. vodka
¾ oz. crème de cacao
Shake and serve in 3 oz. cocktail glass.

POMPIER HIGHBALL (OR VERMOUTH-CASSIS)

3 oz. French vermouth
4 dashes crème de cassis
seltzer
add lemon peel
Serve in highball glass and stir.

COOLER

2 oz. gin
1 cube ice
peel rind of lemon in spiral form
1 split soda
Serve in tall glass and stir.

Most personal preferences in mixed drinks are simply variations on standard or basic themes in much the same manner that all witticisms are supposedly based on seven fundamental joke structures. Carole Landis, for example, swears by a vodka Martini which, if pursued over any length of time, she promises will make the customer scream next morning for a Bloody Mary.

VODKA MARTINI #1

3 oz. vodka
1 oz. dry vermouth
*Stir or spoon with cube ice and serve as a conventional Martini in 4 oz.
glass.*

BLOODY MARY

3 oz. vodka
6 oz. tomato juice
2 dashes Angostura bitters
juice of half lemon
*Shake these together with ice or mix in Waring mixer arid serve cold in
highball glass.*

Monty Woolley improves on the usual proportions of the dry Martini simply
by increasing the conventional proportions of gin and vermouth to four to one,
admonishes barkeeps to use cube ice and no lemon whatsoever, and, when asked
what this will do for the consumer, remarks with a worldly leer: "Consult Lillian
Russell!"

Still another variation on the theme of gin and vermouth, which Cole Porter in
The Two Little Babes in the Woods discovered was the fountain of youth comes
from Mary Astor:

ASTOR PAINLESS ANESTHETIC

3 oz. gin
1 oz. French vermouth
1 oz. Italian vermouth
1 oz. cognac
*Shake well with ice cubes and dash of orange bitters, twist of lemon peel
and just a touch of sugar.*

Don Ameche frowns a masculine frown upon mixed liquor in any form on the
understandable grounds that he is an admirer of straight bourbon whisky and no
nonsense about a chaser. But Bonita Granville offers what she contends to be the
barkeep's answer to the atomic bomb:

SNOW WHITE

5 oz. Southern Comfort
1 oz. vodka
1 oz. fresh pineapple juice
½ oz. orange juice
Mix in a Waring mixer and serve in an old- fashioned glass.

A touch of sentiment attaches to the favorite drink of the ever- provocative Billie Burke Ziegfeld who writes in as follows:

"As I recall, a rather delightful drink Florenz Ziegfeld used to prepare was two-thirds gin and one-third pineapple juice, with the rim of the glass moistened in lemon juice or lime and then twirled in powdered sugar, served very cold. At least he always twirled the first two or three in powdered sugar. After that it didn't matter."

The sworn preference in mixed drinks of John Garfield, and he can be seen whenever in New York giving evidence in the Cub Room to support his testimony, is a Rob Roy or Scotch Manhattan, but Mischa Auer recommends an arrangement which he calls a "Ballalaika" and which, simply enough, depends for its authority on equal parts Cointreau, Vodka and orange juice frapped and served in a cocktail glass. Anne Jeffreys likes a conventional Golden Fizz but with the added attraction of grated cocoanut mixed in it, and Binnie Barnes goes to bat, literally, for a

SCHNORKEL

2 oz. golden bacardi
½ oz. pernod
juice of a large lime
Mix with a little sugar in a Waring mixer and, like the submarine for which the drink is named, you'll be submerged in no time and perhaps going backward to find out where you've been.

It is possible that long before the thirsty reader or patron as the case may be has exhausted this overwhelming catalogue of potables, or vice versa, the inner man or inner woman may be clamoring for solid nutriment and, whether they are served adjacent to the dance floor, in the Cub Room, the Blessed Events Room or elsewhere on the Stork premises, these are a few of the house specialties which make it difficult for Jinx Falkenberg to retain her figure:

FILET MIGNON CAPUCINE

Garnished with broiled stuffed mushrooms, creamed spinach, Bernaiae Sauce.

GUINEA HEM

Breast of Guinea Hen-Saute of garnished asparagus tips. New peas. Madeira Sauce.

TOURNEDAS BALTIMORE

Small Tenderloin Saute with mushrooms smothered with onions. Sliced veal kidney, stewed tomatoes, German fried potatoes.

LAMB CHOP SAINT HILAIRE

Lamb chop stuffed with chicken hash, garnished with sliced green pepper, stewed tomatoes.

MINCED TENDERLOIN OF BEEF A LA DEUTSCH

Sliced Tenderloin, garnished with green peppers. Tartlet of cream corn. Chateau Sauce.

PHEASANT CASSEROLE DERBY

Roast Pheasant stuffed American style. Garnished with dried truffles and foie gras, Madeira Sauce.

ROYAL SQUAB KNICKERBOCKER

Roast Royal Squab in casserole garnished with artichokes. Bottom Parisienne potatoes covered over with chopped hard boiled egg, bread crumbs, and parsley. Madeira Sauce.

SQUAB OF GUINEA HEN—STEVE HANNAGAN

Squab of Guinea Hen, split and saute in butter, garnished with sliced oranges, black cherries. Porto Sauce.

BROILED CHOP OF VENAISON GROUND VENEUR

Broiled chop of Venaison garnished with puree of chestnut, Sauce of Poivrade and currant jelly.

AIGUILETTE OF DUCKLING FLORIDA

Aiguilette of duckling in top of crouton of hominy, garnished with stewed pears, oranges and apples and pineapple. Porto Sauce.

MINUTE STEAK CHEZ TOI

Steak Saute, garnished with diced potatoes, small glace onions and mushrooms.

BREAST OF CHICKEN RIMINI

Breast of chicken-Pique with truffle—serve in crustade. Puree of mushrooms. Supreme Sauce.

SQUAB CHICKEN LOUISIANE

Fried Squab chicken breaded. Garnish with sweet fried potatoes, stewed com, fried bananas Rue Pilaw, Maryland Sauce.

As has been remarked elsewhere in this handbook for eatalls and tosspots of the Fifty-third Street persuasion, nobody in the world drinks all the drinks herein recorded, which is one of God's major mercies, and very few people drink very many of them, but somebody drinks every one of them and what has merit in the sight of any single individual, particularly if he is a notable of this world, is worth passing on for the amusement or instruction of his contemporaries.

Of the several hundred Stork celebrities canvassed in this poll of the flagon-conscious, an overwhelmingly large proportion recorded their preferences as being anything but exotic. Straight bourbon whisky, Scotch and soda, Martini and old-fashioned cocktails pre-dominated on approximately a ten to one basis. A list of the top- drawer names which will vote any time for gin and vermouth against all the confections of all the Harry's New York Bars, Hurricane Bars, Palace Hotels, Ritz Hotels, Gardens of Allah, Pump Rooms and Alibi Bars of the world would stretch from Fifth Avenue to the County Strip, Los Angeles, and would read like an editorial synthesis of *Who's Who, Burke's Peerage*, the

International Motion Picture Almanac, the *Directory of Directors* and the Palm Beach telephone directory.

Then, too, there are old accustomed patrons of Sherman's Shack whose taste for more unusual drinks still follows the conventional bar recipes like Jack Benny, who is a fall guy for Bloody Marys, Ruth Hussey, who dotes on Sazaracs, and Nanette Fabry, who confesses she can take and can't leave Southern Comforts.

Jinx Falkenberg, however, comes up with a Sangrita which she claims is a "favorite with bullfighters in Mexico and me," which is a not too distant relative of claret lemonade:

SANGRITA

2 oz. claret
½ oz. pineapple juice
6 oz. soda
½ oz. lime juice
Mix as a highball, preferably in a tall blue glass like those used at Cesar's Cafe in Tia Juana. Really a temperance drink.

Lilian Harvey likes:

HOCUS-POCUS

2 oz. gin
2 oz. cointreau
2 oz. lemon juice
Frappe and serve in a champagne glass.

James Gleason suggests a nonesuch known as a "Help Wanted Cocktail" comprising equal parts bourbon whisky and apricot brandy, shaken up with a few drops of lemon juice added and adds that in bed is a good place to try it if one has more than three.

Judy Canova, if pressed, will tell you that she likes:

PINK GOODY

1 oz. gin
1 oz. golden bacardi
1 oz. lime juice
Dash of maraschino or grenadine
Serve with crushed ice in a tall highball glass with a generous splash of soda and a stick of pineapple for garnish. After the first drink, she submits, the fruit decoration may be eliminated as unessential.

Andrea King, who confesses that, to date, she has only dared use the formula in half portions and then on an isolated atoll in the South Pacific, recommends:

DEVIL'S TAIL

3 oz. 151 proof Rum
3 oz. vodka
1 oz. lime juice
2 oz. grenadine
To obtain the best results, says Miss King, these should be frapped in a
Waring mixer and served with a float of apricot brandy on top.

Gertrude Niesen asserts that, when thirsty, she does hone and hanker for a conservative little toddy she has dreamed up called a

NIESEN BUZZ-BOMB

1 oz. lime juice
1 oz. Cointreau
1 oz. cognac
1 oz. benedictine
1 oz. vodka
Shake well with crushed ice, strain into a tall highball glass and serve
with a fill-up of the best vintage champagne.

Arthur Berry cannot resist:

RUM BANA

3 oz. Jamaica rum
1 oz. lemon juice
1 tsp. sugar
1 peeled banana
Frappe in a Waring mixer and serve in a broad, flat champagne glass.

And now a few more of the Stork Club's own bar list before we close the bar and retire to the Cub Room for the night.

BARBARY COCKTAIL

¾ oz. Scotch
¾ oz. gin
¾ oz. crème de cacao
½ oz. fresh cream

Shake with shaved ice and serve in Delmonico glass.

EAST INDIA COCKTAIL

1½ oz. brandy
¾ oz. pineapple juice
½ oz. orange curaçao
Decorate with cherry, shake and serve in 3 oz. cocktail glass.

HONEYMOON

1½ oz. applejack
½ oz. benedictine
juice of half lemon
3 dashes curaçao
Shake and serve in 3 oz. cocktail glass.

HAWAII COCKTAIL

1½ oz. gin
1 oz. pineapple juice
1 dash orange bitters
white of egg
Shake and serve in 4 oz. wine glass.

CORONATION COCKTAIL

1½ oz. sherry
1 oz. French vermouth
2 dashes maraschino
3 dashes orange bitters
Stir and serve in a 3 oz. glass.

OJEN COCKTAIL

2 oz. Ojen
1 dash Peychaud bitters
1 tsp. sugar
½ oz. water
Shake and serve in 3 oz. cocktail glass.

MERRY WIDOW

1⅓ oz. gin
1⅓ oz. dubonnet
Twist of lemon peel. Stir and serve in 3 oz. cocktail glass.

SHANDYGAFF

cold beer
cold ginger ale
No ice. Serve in tall glass.

LORRAINE COCKTAIL

1¾ oz. kirsch
½ oz. benedictine
juice of half lime
Shake and serve in 3 oz. cocktail glass.

KANGAROO KICKER

2 oz. vodka
¾ oz. French vermouth
Shake. Twist of lemon peel on top. Serve in 3 oz. cocktail glass.

ARMOUR COCKTAIL

1¾ oz. dry sherry
1 oz. sweet vermouth
twist of lemon peel
Stir and serve in 3 oz. cocktail glass.

R.A.F. COCKTAIL

1¾ oz. applejack
¾ oz. apricot brandy
juice of half lemon
Shake and serve in 3 oz. cocktail glass.

OPAL COCKTAIL

2 oz. absinthe
½ oz. yellow chartreuse
¼ oz. water
Stir and serve in 4 oz. wine glass.

NAPOLEON

2 oz. gin
2 dashes dubonnet
2 dashes Curaçao
2 dashes Fernet Branca
Squeeze lemon peel on top. Shake and serve in 4 oz. wine glass.

AMERICANO HIGHBALL

1 oz. Campari bitters
2 oz. sweet vermouth
Serve in highball glass. Twist of lemon peel. Top with seltzer and stir.

SPRITZER HIGHBALL

Pour 3 oz. chilled Rhine wine in highball glass. One cube of ice. Fill with chilled seltzer.

ALASKA COCKTAIL

2 oz. gin
¾ oz. yellow chartreuse
Stir and serve in 3 oz. cocktail glass.

MOSCOW MULE

2 oz. vodka
1 split ginger beer
crushed ice
Serve in mug and decorate with sprigs of mint.

This volume pretends in no way to the dimensions or erudition of a cellar hook. It is a bar book and as such concerns itself with the simple and essentially naive drinking habits of people in search of comfort, refreshment and the uses of pleasant company rather than the researches of oenophiles and the crafty cellar practices of learned wine stewards.

Ten bottles of champagne are served at the Stork to every one of claret, Burgundy, sauterne or Rhenish for the obvious reason that the pleasures of champagne are immediate to every perceptive sense and that it is a for-fun wine. George Saintsbury might not approve the drinking practices of the Cub Room but he would most assuredly have a good time following them. Mrs. Stuyvesant Fish quite literally floated her way into a reigning position in the New York society of the century's turn by the serving of Niagaras of the very best sparkling wine and other people have done it since. It was Mamie Fish who abolished at her dinners as a tiresome bore the classic service of a variety of wines, each appropriate to its proper course, and served nothing but champagne from soup to dessert with the result that her guests often got to Opera before the end of the second act, an innovation which rocked society to its foundations.

There is no food or time of the day and night when the service and consumption of champagne is not both appropriate and agreeable, a circumstance which attaches to no other beverage yet devised by vintners, brewers or distillers. With the close of hostilities in Europe the products of the great established champagne firms of Rheims and Epernay are again almost universally available in the brands always popular in the United States and England: Bollinger, Veuve Clicquot, Mumm's, Perrier Jouet, Krug, Charles Heidsick, Louis Roederer, Moet and Chandon, Lanson, and a few others of the first importance. The vintages of '33 and '37 will undoubtedly dominate the market for many years to come, but connoisseurs, knowing that wine of vintage quality often is bottled as an undated wine to protect the market, is never impressed by a vintage wine of second quality when he finds on the card such numbers as Krug's Private Cuvee, Bollinger Brut or Perrier-Jouet Dry England. The sans annee wine is often a very superior product indeed with the added inducement that it is usually a couple of dollars cheaper than the vintage years whose prices are jealously and zealously maintained at high levels by shippers, dealers and restaurateurs alike.

Aside from champagnes, New York's taste in table wines runs almost exclusively to claret and Burgundy and the German wines of the Rhine. Bordeaux (claret) generally is regarded as less pre-tentious than the classic vintages of Burgundy, and white Bordeaux or sauternes enjoy a certain vogue with the service of fish and luncheon dishes of a light nature. True Chablis, the aristocrat of white still wines, is so difficult to obtain as this is being written as to be inconsiderable in this brief footnote.

Since discussions of the merits, qualities and service of even one of the classes of wine mentioned have over several centuries engaged the attentions of many learned men and have supplied the matter for innumerable and ponderous books, it will be seen that any detailed mention of them, let alone so chancy a subject as an estimate of current vintages, is impracticable in the extreme, as well as outside the province of this book.

As has been the case with the vintages of the grape, it is not the purpose of this bar book to trespass upon the provinces which are more properly those of a cellar book, and brandies in all their redactions, classifications and varieties of wonder are more properly the concerns of a sommelier than of a barkeep. With the exceptions of a few formulas, they are unsuited to use in mixed drinks, being an essence for the consideration of the mature palate and the discretion of experience. Brandy is the drink for heroes and it is also the drink for scholars. Even the brashest barkeep hesitates at the command of a patron for a pedigreed Cognac to be used in a stinger or rendered in highball form with soda water.

Many and learned books have been devoted to Cognac and its allied or related eaux de vie and the Stork stocks a supply that is the wonder and pleasure of the knowing and the undoing of the un- judicious, for a great Cognac has about it a pantherlike treachery in that its absorption seems quite devoid of dismaying results until next day or even next week. It possesses, too, the humorous attribute of deluding the consumer into the belief that he is entirely sober until he finds himself, like David Copperfield at his first wine dinner, unaccountably face down on the stair landing and enquiring of kind friends who it might have been that has so rudely fallen.

Only research and a considerable investment of time and patience can fairly determine an individual taste in Cognacs and the experts will dispute the matter until Judgment Day. Its frequently low alcoholic content should never be taken as an index of its chemical and toxic strength and some of the most perilous of all Fines of great age may be no more than thirty-six or forty percent alcohol. Personally the taste of the author runs to a Cognac or Fine Champagne approximately forty years old, an age when the brands and blends of all accredited houses are possessed of common and often indistinguishable qualities of even mellowness without too great a strain on their essential strength and vitality. In common practice the stars on Cognac should indicate approximately three years of age.

The initials by which Cognacs are classified vary with different firms of export but, again, generally speaking, they may be interpreted as follows:

E: Especial
F: Fine
V: Very
O: Old
S: Superior
P: Pale
X: Extra
C: Cognac

Thus it will be seen that a VSOP is, within the honor of the distiller and his established reputation for an honest description of his product, a Very Superior Old Pale Cognac, but none of these adjectives has any formal definition or meaning beyond the discretion of the firm which uses it. In the realm of commercial Cognacs the names Hennessy, Hines, Denis Mounier and a few others are more to be trusted than many stars and all the initials which customarily follow the names of British admirals.

The entire matter of after dinner liqueurs resolves itself into one of personal taste and preference and neither advice nor instructions in their use seem altogether valid. The sweet, highly aromatic cordial, generally speaking, is a survival of a more florid and rococo age of drinking and manners, and their use in the United States at the moment is almost entirely confined to infusion in mixed drinks, hut it doesn't take any graybeard to recall a period when they were held in high and universal esteem and their service in elaborate profusion was a hallmark of gentility and sophistication.

The trans-Atlantic liners of twenty-five years ago were probably the last great stronghold of the liqueur. At the same time no dinner in London or Paris was complete without the appearance of an almost overwhelming variety of sweet cordials with flavors deriving from every known flower and herb and a few unheard of by anyone: Benedictine, Chartreuse, Cointreau, Kümmel, Curaçao, Triple Sec, Crème de Cacao, Crème de Cassis, Maraschino, Prunella, Peach Brandy, Grand Marnier, Danziger Goldwasser, Flora Delle Alpi, Kirsch, Drambuie, Anise and Swedish Punch. They came in every variety of bottle, tall, squat and flattened, globular, square, octagonal, fluted, beribboned, chaste and plain, austere and fanciful.

Today the run of liqueurs has subsided almost to the vanishing point although a green or white mint frappe or glass of Cointreau is occasionally seen.

Nine Americans out of ten who do not order a highball after dinner call for Cognac, American brandy, Armagnac or one of the related eaux de vie of the family of grape spirits.

It is with the greatest infrequency, nowadays, that private drinking parties or groups of night club guests of modest size command the preparation of the elaborate communal punches, grogs, eggnogs and sangarees which a century ago were the staples in all public taverns and ordinaries. Large quantities of punch are still in vogue for weddings, receptions and other formal occasions where their purpose is partly as refreshment, partly for ornament and the sake of tradition. The punchbowl as such has largely disappeared from public bars, although the author can well remember when an enormous bath of Adams House Punch was set out every morning on the bar of that once wonderful hotel in Boston and was a day-long favorite with tarriers at the Washington Street entry of Calvin Coolidge's favorite hotel.

These more or less elaborate drinks, most of which have one variety of rum or another for the base, are, however, still popular in individual service and the closer one gets to the tropics the more frequently one encounters such standards of hot country drinking as Planter's Punch, Fish House Punch, rum swizzle and gin coolers. The most celebrated of all American regional drinks, the Mint Julep, is, in actual fact, a highly concentrated individual serving of Bourbon Whisky Punch.

Of the several score punches in the bright and heady lexicon of the Stork Club the following are the elaborate mixed drinks most in requisition in the ordinary course of the seasons:

ROMAN PUNCH

1 tsp. sugar
juice of half lemon
juice of half orange
white of egg, beaten
2 oz. rum
Shake well. Fill goblet with chilled champagne.

CLARET PUNCH

3 oz. claret
juice of half lemon
2 dashes curaçao
1 tsp. sugar
Dress with fruit and serve in goblet with fine ice, squirt of seltzer.

BRANDY PUNCH

2 oz. brandy
sugar to taste
1 dash grenadine
1 dash maraschino
shaved ice
Use goblet. Dress with mint and fruit. Stir well. Squirt of seltzer.

SAUTERNE PUNCH

(for 1 gallon)
juice of five lemons
2 ponies brandy
1 pony applejack
1½ oz. pineapple juice

2 dashes yellow chartreuse
2 qt. sauterne
2 qt. sparkling water
Sugar to taste. Cucumber rinds. Dress with fruit.

PIMM'S #1

2 cubes of ice
slice of lemon
cucumber rind
lemon soda
2 oz. Pimm's No. 1
Serve in tall glass and stir.

WHISKY PUNCH

2 oz. whisky
juice of half lemon
1 tsp. sugar
shaved ice
Use goblet. Dress with fruit. Squirt of seltzer.

BRANDY RICKEY

1½ oz. brandy
juice of half lime and rind
1 cube ice
Stir and serve in highball glass. Fill glass with seltzer.

CRUSTAS

2 oz. Jamaica rum
juice of one lime
½ tsp. sugar
3 dashes maraschino
2.dashes Angostura bitters
Shake. Sugar rim of glass. Peel of half orange in Tom Collins glass.
  Cracked ice to the top and fill with soda. Decorate with fruit and serve
  with straws.

POUSSE-CAFÉ

⅙ oz. grenadine (red color)
⅙ oz. crème de cacao (black color)
⅙ oz. maraschino (white color)
⅙ oz. orange curaçao (orange color)
⅙ oz. crème Yvette (violet color)
⅙ oz. brandy (amber color)
Pour in the order named very carefully and slowly in cordial glasses to prevent cloudiness.

PEACH VELVET

insert raw peach in peach champagne glass
fill with chilled champagne
1 dash peach brandy on top

RUM COBBLER

2 oz. rum
1 dashes lemon juice
2 tsp. sugar
dash of cherry brandy
Shake and decorate with fruit, sprig of mint.

RUM PUNCH

juice of half lemon
1 tsp. sugar
2 oz. rum
1 dash brandy
Fruit. Serve in goblet with fine ice.

GLÖGG-HOT WINE DRINK

¾ cup sugar
2 oz. Angostura bitters
1 pint sherry wine
1 pint claret wine
½ pint brandy

Use large flame proof casserole. Place over fire until piping hot. Serve in old-fashioned glass or mug. (Serves fifteen.)

In the Stork Club's repertory of more exotic drinks and one which calls for some special notice because of its antecedents and background is certainly the Blue Blazer. As in the cases of the Sidecar and the Gibson, the originator of the Blue Blazer is known to the record, and historical research has disclosed that the arrangement in all its Paine's Fireworks splendor was first produced—perhaps detonated would be a better word—by Professor Jerry Thomas, a celebrated bar-keep of the last century, while working at the El Dorado, a San Francisco oasis of wide repute, in 1849.

Professor Thomas, who stemmed from New Haven, where he had practiced since early manhood on the nearly impregnable persons of Yale undergraduates, was famous as a practitioner who could gentle the most voracious drinker fresh from the placer diggings of Hangtown, and one evening his talents were put to the ultimate test. A whiskered giant, booted to the hips and clattering with Colt's patent firearms, demanded satisfaction. "Fix me," he roared, "some hell-fire that will shake me right down to my gizzard."

Professor Thomas consulted his files, his assistants, and then, while the word spread throughout Geary Street that great doings were afoot and crowds gathered, he prepared to do his stuff. First he set upon the bar (according to Herbert Asbury, the learned historian of Americana) the two silver mugs, imported from New York around the Horn, that were the show utensils of the El Dorado.

"Gentlemen," he announced. "You are about to witness the birth of a new beverage!"

"A sigh of anticipation arose from the assemblage," writes Mr. Asbury in recording the occasion, "and with one accord the mass of men moved forward until they stood, respectfully, five deep before the bar, the whiskered giant, still booted, in the front rank. Professor Thomas smiled and quietly poured a tumbler of Scotch whisky into one of the mugs, followed by a slightly smaller quantity of boiling water. Then with an evil smelling sulphur match, he ignited the liquid and, as the blue flame shot toward the ceiling and the crowd fell back in awe, he hurled the blazing mixture back and forth between the two mugs, with a rapidity and dexterity that was well nigh unbelievable. This amazing spectacle continued in full movement for perhaps ten seconds, and then Professor Thomas poured the beverage into a tumbler and smothered the flame. He stirred a spoonful of pulverized white sugar into the mixture, added a twist of lemon peel, and shoved the smoking concoction across to the booted and spurred giant.

"'Sir,' said Professor Thomas, bowing, 'The Blue Blazer!'

"The boastful miner threw back his head and flung the boiling drink down his throat. He stood motionless for a moment, smacking his lips and tasting the full flavor of it, and then a startled expression spread over his face. He swayed like a reed in the wind. He shivered from head to foot. His teeth rattled. He batted his eyes. His mouth opened and closed; he could say nothing. Then he sank slowly into a chair. He was no longer fit to be tied."[*]

BLUE BLAZER

1 wine glass Scotch whisky
1 wine glass boiling water

Use two large silver-plated mugs with handles. Put the whisky into one mug and the boiling water into the other, ignite the whisky with fire, and while blazing mix both ingredients by pouring them four or five times from one mug to the other. If well done this will have the appearance of a continued stream of liquid fire. Sweeten with powdered sugar and serve in a small bar tumbler with a piece of lemon peel.

While possessed of neither the spectacular nor the fire hazard qualities of the masterpiece devised by Professor Thomas, there are several other arrangements dependent upon the skill and artistry of the barkeep or cellarman for their effectiveness rather than their alcoholic content alone:

BRANDY CAPRICE

Make an incision around center of orange. Carefully pull skin back towards one end so as to form a cup and still be fastened to orange. Pour ½ oz. of brandy and ignite. While burning, slowly pass one lump of sugar in a teaspoon through flame until sugar melts. Stir.

TOM AND JERRY

1 whole egg
1 tsp. sugar
1½ oz. Jamaica rum

Beat up yolk and white of egg separately. Then mix the yolk and white together. Use stem glass or China mug, adding the spirits, then, fill with boiling water. Dash of brandy. Top with nutmeg. Serve in Tom & Jerry mug.

MAJOR BAILEY

2 oz. gin
4 dashes lemon juice

---

[*] *From* The Bon Vivant's Companion, *edited by Herbert Asbury, ©1927, 1928 by Alfred A. Knopf, Inc. and reprinted by permission of the publishers.*

1 tsp. sugar
crushed mint
shaved ice
Serve in silver mug or tall glass. Stir very well until mug is frosted.
   Decorate with sprigs of mint and serve with straws.

SINGAPORE SLING

2 oz. gin
¾ oz. cherry brandy
1 dash benedictine
juice of lemon
Serve in tall glass with 2 cubes of ice. Decorate with slice of orange and
   sprig of mint. Top with carbonic.

CAFÉ AU KIRSCH

1½ oz. kirsch
1 tsp. sugar
white of egg
add coffee
Shake and serve in wine glass.

AFTER-DINNER COCKTAIL

1 oz. prunella brandy
1 oz. cherry brandy
dash lemon juice
Shake and serve in 4 oz. wine glass.

B AND B

½ oz. benedictine
½ oz. brandy
Serve in cordial glass.

TROPICAL COCKTAIL

¾ oz. crème de cacao
1¼ oz. French vermouth

¾ oz. maraschino
1 dash orange bitters
Shake well and serve in 4 oz. wine glass.

CHAMPAGNE PUNCH (FOR 1 GALLON)

2 qt. champagne
1 pony maraschino
3 ponies brandy
1 pony Curaçao
1 dash yellow chartreuse
juice of four lemons
2 qt. sparkling water
sugar to taste
fruit
block of ice

ROCKY MOUNTAIN COOLER

1 egg
1 tsp. simple syrup
4 dashes Angostura bitters
juice of one lemon
6 oz. cider
*Put ingredients into shaker, add cracked ice sufficient and shake
thoroughly. Strain into 10 oz. glass. Dust with nutmeg, serve with
straws.*

ZOOM

1½ oz. brandy
¼ oz. honey
½ oz. fresh cream
Shake and serve in 4 oz. wine glass.

HOT BUTTERED RUM

1½ oz. Jamaica rum
1 lump sugar
1 small slice butter

4 cloves
Use an old-fashioned glass or mug. Fill with boiling water. Stir.

SANGAREE

3 oz. port or sherry wine
1 tsp. sugar
cracked ice
slice of lemon
Fill glass with water. Serve in Tom Collins glass. Nutmeg on top. Stir.

Which brings us inevitably to the controversial and endlessly embattled subject of what, for all its association in the popular imagination with the south and southern chivalry, is probably the nearest thing extant to the American national drink, the classic of classics, the colonel's delight, a snare and engine of destruction for the unwary, the ever changing yet immutable and changeless mint julep.

The fallacious belief that adequate juleps cannot be served, obtained or appreciated anywhere north of, at the very extremity of geographic possibility, Baltimore, has long since vanished in the face of overwhelming evidence to the contrary. The julep can and does flourish, green-bay-tree like, within the boundaries of Manhattan and, more specifically and even more handily for present purposes, in Fifty-third Street not a seltzer squirt from Fifth Avenue.

Space, the informed intelligence of the author and the patience of thirsty readers all militate against any prolonged discussion of the several and various aspects of juleps. The author has hoisted them gratefully in silver chalices of half quart capacity in Maysville, Kentucky, overlooking the incomparable vista of the Ohio as the Chesapeake and Ohio's "George Washington" has rolled down the valley at summer dusk. He has lifted them in the perfumed precincts of a springtime garden in Charleston in little gold toddy mugs that were prized in the family still owning them when gentlemen wore court swords on the street and satin breeches and silver buckled pumps were taken for granted. He has drunk drastic juleps in Natchez-Above-the-Levee that made him wonder how the Mississippi packet gamblers of the fifties with their skirted coats and the Remington derringers concealed in lace cuffs could see a hand of cards. And he has accepted juleps that were a sacrament in old walled gardens in New Orleans while the sailors fought fistfights and the town tarts paraded the ill-lit and uneven pavements of Royal Street nearby.

All the juleps were good. Some seemed better than others, but that was only because the others had been drunk first.

Let, as in the *Rubaiyat*, the "four and seventy jarring sects" dispute the merits of crushed ice and shaved ice, of pounded mint, muddled mint and only bruised mint (adjectives which so often lend themselves equally handily to the julep drinkers themselves) and the virtue of just a small slug of overproof Jamaica rum floating on top of the whole creation. This is the Stork julep and it has stayed and strengthened many brave men and fair women, confirming them in the almost irrefutable belief that most of the good things of the world come in glass bottles and that the very best of them say bourbon on the outside:

MINT JULEP

2 oz. bourbon
1 tsp. sugar
4 sprigs mint

Mash with muddler. Fill the silver mug with shaved ice. Stir until the outside of the mug is frosted. Decorate with sprigs of mint and serve with straws. Add green cherry.

Personally, the author cleaves to a slight variance of the foregoing: four ounces of Jack Daniel's proof bourbon with a float of two ounces of Hines' Triomph Cognac on top.

Officer, please back the patrol wagon nearer the curb; the step is too high for my mother.

AN APPENDIX OF DRINKS SUGGESTED BY MEMBERS OF THE STAFF OF THE STORK CLUB

Anyone who peruses the content of this bar book will discover that, integrated in its editorial economy, are a number of drink suggestions and recipes originating with patrons of the Stork and differing in more or less degree from the nearest related and established drink. As the devising of new and more fascinating ways of insinuating alcohol and the pleasant humors that accompany its proper absorption into the human system is by no means confined to guests, it was thought by the author a shrewd notion to solicit some recipes by members of the staff.

The gustatory ruffles and flourishes in this appendix are the brain children of various members of Mr. Billingsley's staff, and they are included as evidence of its versatility in the practice of the useful arts and sciences.

Most of them originate with Nathaniel Cook, the chief barman, but almost everyone, from Eddie Whittmer and Harry Kaye, the captains, to Veronica Harrold, who holds hats prettily for ransom at the door, wanted in, and here are their contributions to the practical humanities.

Cookie's secret archives contain the following:

SPIKER COCKTAIL

⅓ oz. green crème de menthe
⅔ oz. imported brandy
Serve in 3 oz. cocktail glass, well chilled.
Shake well and strain.

STORK CLUB COOLER

1 tsp. sugar
juice of half orange
2 oz. gin
Serve in 12 oz. Collins glass and shake well and strain into glass with
shaved ice and serve decorated with fruit and straws.

EYE-OPENER

1 oz. pineapple juice
dash maraschino
1½ oz. brandy
Shake and strain. Serve in 3 oz. cocktail glass.

BOURBON SOCIETY

1 oz. bourbon
Serve in an old-fashioned glass with 6 or 8 tiny ice cubes and a twist of
  dropped lemon peel.

F.B.I. FIZZ

½ oz. Cherry Heering brandy
½ oz. bourbon
½ oz. Jamaica rum
twist orange peel
Serve in 8 oz. highball glass. Shake well and strain into glass with two ice
  cubes and top with soda water.

DETROIT DAISY

dash grenadine
juice of one lime
2 oz. rum (dark)
add fresh mint leaves
Serve in 12 oz. Collins glass. Shake hard. Strain into glass filled with
  shaved ice. Decorate with sprig of mint and green cherry.

BLINKER COCKTAIL

dash grenadine
¾ oz. grapefruit juice
1½ oz. rye whisky
Shake well and strain. Serve in 3 oz. cocktail glass.

Arthur Berry, a captain of waiters, donates the specifications for:

KICKING COW

⅓ oz. maple syrup
⅓ cream
⅔ oz. bourbon or rye
Shake well and use cracked ice. Serve in a cocktail glass.
And the following are the dream children of Eddie Whittmer:

EDITH DAY COCKTAIL

white of one egg
¾ jigger of grapefruit juice
1 jigger of dry gin
½ tsp. sugar
Serve in a champagne glass, well frapped.

WILDFLOWER COCKTAIL

1 dash of grenadine
¾ jigger grapefruit juice
1 jigger of Scotch whisky
Serve in a hollow stem champagne glass, well trapped.

BLESSED EVENT

juice of half lime
dash of curaçao
2 oz. benedictine
2 oz. applejack
Shake and strain. Serve in cocktail glass.

BROOKLYNITE

dash of lime juice
½ oz. of honey
2 oz. Jamaica rum
dash of Angostura bitters
Shake well and strain. Serve in 3 oz. cocktail glass.

STORK CLUB COCKTAIL

dash of lime juice
juice of half orange
dash of triple sec
1½ oz. gin
dash of Angostura bitters
Shake well and strain in chilled 4 oz. glass.

SALTY DOG COLLINS

juice of one lime
¼ tsp. salt
1½ oz. gin
Shake in a cocktail shaker and pour into 10 oz. glass with two ice cubes.

CUFF AND BUTTONS

juice of half lime
4 dashes of sweet vermouth
2 oz. Southern Comfort
Shake in a cocktail shaker, strain and serve chilled in 3 oz. glass.

4TH ESTATE COCKTAIL

⅓ oz. French vermouth
⅓ oz. Italian vermouth
⅓ oz. gin
4 dashes absinthe
*Stir well and strain into 3 oz. cocktail glass. Add cherry and twist
    lemon peel.*

DEBUTANTE'S DREAM

⅓ oz. bourbon
⅓ oz. brandy
⅓ oz. orange juice
dash of lemon juice
Shake well and strain. Serve in 3 oz. cocktail glass.

MR. NEW YORKER

1¾ oz. French vermouth
½ oz. gin
½ oz. dry sherry
dash of Cointreau
Stir and strain. Serve in 3 oz. cocktail glass.

QUEENS TASTE COCKTAIL

⅓ oz. French vermouth
⅔ oz. gin
few leaves of fresh crushed mint
Stir and strain. Serve in chilled 3 oz. cocktail glass.

ORCHID COCKTAIL

dash crème Yvette
white of one egg
2 oz. gin
Serve in chilled 4 oz. wine glass. Shake hard and strain. Use only a dash of crème Yvette. It will produce a delightful violet flavor, with a coloring as nice as an orchid flower.

A DREAM COCKTAIL

dash of triple sec
dash of lime juice
dash cream
1½ oz. gin
Shake and strain. Serve in 3 oz. cocktail glass.

Albert Coleman, one of Cookie's vicars at the bar has evolved:

WALLY COCKTAIL

⅓ oz. lime juice
⅓ oz. peach brandy
⅓ oz. applejack
Shake well. Serve in a cocktail glass.

GOLDEN SLIPPER

1 pony of yellow chartreuse
1 yolk of egg
1 pony of goldwasser
Pour one pony of yellow chartreuse into sherry glass. Then drop yolk of
egg without breaking it and then add one pony of goldwasser on top.

YELLOW PARROT

⅓ oz. absinthe
½ oz. yellow chartreuse
⅓ oz. apricot brandy
Shake well. Serve in a cocktail glass.

ZARANES COCKTAIL

⅓ oz. vodka
½ oz. apricot brandy
dash of Angostura bitters
Shake well. Serve in a cocktail glass.

BRANDY SMASH

⅓ tsp. sugar
1 squirt of seltzer
4 sprigs of mint
1 wine glass of brandy
Serve in a champagne glass. Fill with fine ice, stir well with a spoon. Press
the mint to extract the essence as in a julep. Decorate with berries
or fruit.

DAILY DOUBLE C

1 oz. rum
1 oz. Italian vermouth
2 cherries
Mix with ice and stir. Serve in a cocktail glass.

From Julius Corsani, barman, come the "Julius Special" and "Rum Scoundrel":

JULIUS SPECIAL

⅓ oz. lime juice
⅓ oz. cointreau
⅔ oz. Jamaica rum—3 Daggers
Serve in a cocktail glass.

RUM SCOUNDREL

⅓ oz. lime juice
⅔ oz. white or gold bacardi rum
1 tsp. sugar
Serve in an old-fashioned glass. Rub the edge of the glass with lemon and
dip in sugar to coat it.

The nominations of Donald Arden, chief of Mr. Billingsley's staff of publicists, are:

GOLDEN PANTHER (FOR THREE)

2 oz. gin
2 oz. brandy
2 oz. whisky
1 oz. dry vermouth
juice of half orange
Serve in 6 oz. glass. Pour ingredients into a shaker with cracked ice. Shake
well and pour into individual glasses

ALL AMERICAN PUNCH (30 PERSONS)

15 oz. Southern Comfort
5 bottles Coca-Cola
3 6-oz. bottles soda
1 oz. cherry juice
5 oranges
3 lemons
2 limes
12 cherries
Dice cherries into small pieces and squeeze the oranges and lemons and
limes. Pour into punch bowl and add Coca-Cola, soda, cherry juice,
and Southern Comfort. Add shaven and crushed ice to chill thoroughly.
Stir until chilled. Serve in a chilled punch glass.

According to the sworn testimony of Joe Acre, captain, the vodka Martini is a favorite with Dashiel Hammett:

VODKA MARTINI #2

⅓ oz. French vermouth
⅔ oz. vodka
Serve in a cocktail glass. Serve very cold.

While Leo Spitzel, captain, asserts that a "Stratosphere Cocktail" will do wonders for you:

STRATOSPHERE COCKTAIL

glass of champagne
¾ oz. crème Yvette
Serve in a champagne glass. Add a few dashes of crème Yvette to
    champagne until purple colored. Add two pieces of dove and serve very
    cold.

Frank Harris, the door captain, favors a "Franko-Ra":

FRANKO-RA

1 oz. white bacardi
⅔ oz. orange juice
⅓ oz. lemon juice
tsp. of sugar
Shake well. Serve in a cocktail glass.

Edward G. Johnson, a captain, urges customers on to a "Frozen Strawberry Daiquiri":

FROZEN STRAWBERRY DAIQUIRI

1½ oz. Daiquiri rum
1½ oz. lemon juice
3 or 4 ripe strawberries
small spoonful of sugar
Serve in a champagne glass. Make in the same manner as the usual frozen
    Daiquiri in the Waring mixer. It should come out with a nice color.

While Arnold Sanchez, of the bar staff, assails the Gringo palates with a "South of the Border":

SOUTH OF THE BORDER LONGTAIL

1 oz. Southern Comfort
6 oz. milk
½ tsp. sugar
1 banana
nutmeg
Serve in a Tom Collins glass. Put ingredients in a frozen Daiquiri mixer with little shaved ice for one minute.

And Ernest Luthi, captain, recommends a "French Daiquiri"

FRENCH DAIQUIRI

½ oz. lime juice
⅔ oz. bacardi rum
a little sugar
dash of cassis
few fresh mint leaves
Shake well. Serve in a cocktail glass.

Another of Ernest's creations in considerable requisition is a

SPECIAL

fresh lemon juice
sugar
rye
dash apricot brandy
Shake well. Serve in a cocktail glass. In the summer, the whole contents of the shaker may be emptied into a Tom Collins glass, filled with soda, and served as a long, refreshing and cooling drink.

And a cure for butterflies in the stomach is offered by Fred Armour, the house manager:

BUTTERFLIES COCKTAIL

¼ oz. lemon juice
¼ oz. grenadine
½ oz. applejack

¼ oz. gin
shaved ice
Shake well and then strain. Serve in a cocktail glass.

One of the Club's favorite waiters who is simply known as "Mr. Valentine" supplies the secret of:

THE SWISS YODELER

1 fresh lime
1 tsp. of molasses
½ tsp. of granulated sugar
1½ oz. bacardi rum
Serve in a chilled cocktail glass.

Joe Acre, the captain, persuades the customers with a "Palmetto":

PALMETTO COCKTAIL

¼ oz. cointreau
¼ oz. apricot brandy
¼ oz. light rum
¼ oz. lemon juice
Serve in a cocktail glass.

The literary touch is supplied by an "Arch of Triumph Cocktail" which is suggested by Lisa Lee, the Stork receptionist, inspired by the capacity for Calvados of the characters in the Remarque novel:

ARCH OF TRIUMPH COCKTAIL

⅔ calvados
⅓ lemon juice
1 tsp. sugar
Stir in cocktail shaker. Shake well and serve in cocktail glass.

An "Ann Sheridan Cocktail" is the gift of Harry Kaye, the urbane waiter captain of the Cub Room:

ANN SHERIDAN COCKTAIL

juice of half lime and leave the skin in mixer
⅓ oz. of orange curaçao
⅔ oz. white bacardi rum
Shake well and serve in a cocktail glass.

While a brisk sock from the distaff side is added by Veronica Harrold of the hat checking department:

STAY UP LATE

½ oz. lemon juice
½ oz. club soda
2 oz. gin
½ oz. brandy
little sugar
lemon slice
Serve in a Collins glass.

Alice Henry, of the Billingsley office staff, offers the "Romance Cocktail"; and the "Victory," both of which originated in Paris during the first world war:

ROMANCE COCKTAIL

½ oz. brandy (cognac) and curaçao mixed in equal parts
½ oz. Amer-Picon
½ oz. French vermouth
½ oz. Italian vermouth
Add cracked ice and shake. Serve in a cock- tail glass.

VICTORY

½ oz. orange and lemon juice mixed in
equal parts with several dashes of grenadine
1 oz. French vermouth
1 oz. Italian vermouth
Add cracked ice and shake. Serve in a cocktail glass.

The "Pink Top" is the creation of Mario Bellettini, a captain:

PINK TOP

1½ oz. gin
¾ oz. grand maraier
¼ oz. lemon juice
dash grenadine
Shake well and serve very cold.

While at the end of the procession comes the contribution of Kittie Kincaid of the hat room:

WHISKEY SOUR ON THE SWEET SIDE

1 oz. rye
½ oz. lemon juice
Serve with cherry, orange and sugar.

And Albert Butrice's "Round Robin" from behind the bar:

ROUND ROBIN

white of one egg
tsp. of sugar
1 oz. absinthe
1 oz. brandy
Shake well. Serve in a still wine glass.

And finally Tony Malinary's "Ranger Cocktail":

RANGER COCKTAIL

⅓ oz. rum (light)
⅓ oz. gin
⅓ oz. lemon juice
sugar to sweeten
Shake well. Serve in cocktail glass.

Throw a Stork Club Party

Shermane Billingsley

DEAR FRIENDS

So Many of You Have Written such wonderful letters to me over the years, sharing your memories of the Stork Club. "I had my 'Sweet Sixteen' party at the Stork!" "Dad proposed to Mom while dancing in the Shermane Suite!" "My father's first stop in New York after returning from World War II was the Cub Room!" "My sister and I still remember the scent of our mother's perfume as she kissed us good night before leaving for the Stork Club!" Still others wrote that they never had the opportunity to visit the Stork Club but collected the original black-and-white Stork ashtrays and other memorabilia because it helped them feel a part of it.

Most of your letters ended with a request: Would I please help you create a Stork Club party for a special occasion? Birthday? (Celeste Holm always celebrated hers there!) Engagement? (Grace Kelly and Prince Rainier announced their engagement in the Cub Room.) Easter? (Burt Lahr, Irving Berlin, Bing Crosby, and John Jacob Astor all brought their children to the Stork Club.) New Year's Eve? (Picture J. Edgar Hoover, Mary Martin, Fred Astaire, and Ginger Rogers, dressed in their finest, donning paper party hats!) This book has given me the perfect opportunity to help you plan your dream event at your very own Stork Club, whether it's a specially designated part of your home or a banquet hall booked for the night.

I learned from the best by watching and listening as my father, Sherman, personally took charge of every detail involved in planning his fabulous events. Some children learn at their father's knee; in my case, I was perched on top of Table 50 in the Cub Room as soon as I could sit up! In fact, I still cherish a photo taken of me when I was about nine months old, seated on Table 50 with my father and Walter Winchell nervously flanking me to make sure that I didn't tumble off!

Table 50 was in the entrance corner of the Cub Room and seated up to ten people. It afforded a view of all who came and went. It was the first choice of everyone, from Marilyn Monroe and Joe DiMaggio to J. Edgar Hoover. But it was also the family table. No matter which celebrities were expected, Table 50 was reserved for my mother, my sisters, and me every Thanksgiving, Christmas, and Easter. It is where my memories of growing up at the Stork Club begin and end. Over the years, it was where pictures were taken of me with my childhood heroes: Hopalong Cassidy, Roy Rogers, the Cisco Kid, and even Rin-Tin-Tin!

One special photograph was taken of me with James Arness when he was starring as Marshall Matt Dillon on *Gunsmoke*. I was a big fan of *Gunsmoke* and had a huge crush on James Arness. But one year, it was on opposite my father's *Stork Club* television show and my mother forbade me to watch any other program when my father's show was on. Now, I dearly loved my father and, as you know, often appeared on *The Stork Club* show. But I really preferred to watch *Gunsmoke*! Mother was horrified, and we had quite a row about it; she considered it traitorous to choose anything that competed with the Stork Club—on any level!

Until I was six or seven years old, my nanny, Nellie Fitzgerald, would take me to the Stork Club every afternoon around 4 P.M. to visit my father. Sometimes my father would order a plate of stew or a bowl of rice pudding. More often, he would opt for his usual ⅓ coffee, ⅓ milk, and ½ hot water, while Nanny had tea and pastry and I ordered banana ice cream in a tall glass of ginger ale.

I was never bored. As my father kept a stash of gifts for his guests' children. I was often surprised with a new coloring book and crayons, a Trudy doll (a knob turned the head and changed the facial expression), or some other toy. Between lunch and dinner the club was usually not busy, so my father would go up to his seventh-floor suite and bring down one of the pets that my mother would not allow in our home: my guinea pig, parrot, or rhesus monkey.

I have always related to Eloise of the Plaza because when I could escape from my nanny, I would rush upstairs to the ladies' room, lock all the cubicles from the inside, and crawl out. That meant having to find the skinniest busboy to go up and unlock them when Dorothy Kilgallen and her mother stopped by one afternoon after shopping.

By the time I was ten, my father would pick me up every day after school at 3 P.M. Together we would walk from the school on East Ninety-first Street to the Stork Club on East Fifty-third Street. I treasured those walks because I had my father's undivided attention, and we talked about what we had done during the day. Once at the Stork Club, we sat at my father's table. I had graduated from banana ice cream in ginger ale to Steak Diane (recipe to follow) and a Coke, but my father's afternoon snacks remained unchanged. By 4 P.M. we were often joined by his associates and friends, stopping by for early cocktails with perhaps a touch of business mixed in. I still remember sitting there as Roy Cohn and my father dis cussed legal strategies. Sometimes the visitors joining us were more glamorous: Clare Boothe Luce, the senior editors of *Vogue*, or the top executives from Elizabeth Arden's Red Door Salon, to name a few.

On my first date, around age fifteen, my father insisted that I bring the young man to the Stork Club and seated us at Table 50. As we were preparing to leave, he said, in easy earshot of my date: "Now, you know what to do if he tries to kiss you. You punch him in the stomach, and when he doubles over, you sock him in the jaw!" Needless to say, I received not the slightest suggestion of a kiss; but amazingly, the young man continued to call for many years and, as with a number of other men that I dated, grew quite fond of my father.

For over twenty years I watched in awe as my father went about planning and hosting fabulous events. I have distilled all that he taught me into three basic principles: prepare, make your guests feel special, and relax! If you follow these fundamental rules, each of you can be your own Sherman Billingsley and throw a memorable Stork Club party in your home, a restaurant, or a banquet hall.

SHERMAN'S RULE #1:

Prepare!

My father put in at least sixteen hours every day making sure that the food was made from the finest ingredients, the silver polished, the salt and pepper shakers filled, the flowers fresh, and the staff respectful and ready for anything. You must begin by determining the size of the Stork Club party you want to have. Is it an intimate dinner party for a group of eight to ten (the Cub Room)? A fun-filled baby shower for twenty-five to thirty (the Blessed Event Room)? A New Year's Eve gala for fifty to sixty (the Shermane Suite)? Once you have a sense of the size of your party, consider the location. Can you host the event in your home? If not, find a restaurant or banquet hall that you can work with to recreate the ambience of the original Stork Club.

You will be fine using plain white tablecloths. Sometimes the Stork Club tablecloths had a green border. If that's your preference, just use a dark green Magic Marker to draw the border on the skirt. To be authentic, make sure that each table has a bowl of iced olives, radishes, scallions, and celery hearts, as well as a basket of French rolls. The wooden stork bud-vase holders have become collectors' items, but a bowl of red roses as a centerpiece is right out of the original Stork Club. The black-and-white ashtrays are also scarce, but if you don't personally own one, someone you know probably has one to lend you.

As for glasses and flatware, keep it simple. Shortly after the club closed (the family and "steadies" always called it "the club"), I had a call from a restaurateur saying that the then "junior" Rockefellers, Hearsts, and Astors wanted to open a new Stork Club. They asked me for some advice, as well as my endorsement. When I heard their ideas about Baccarat glasses and sterling flatware, I suggested they lie down until the feeling passed. When you are feeding two thousand patrons a day, you keep everything sparkling but sturdy and do not create the temptation for theft—unless it's good advertising for you.

SHERMAN'S RULE #2:

Make Your Guests feel Special!

Start with the concept of the gold chain. Create your own Stork Club gold chain by hooking together two or three gold-plated link belts and stringing it across the entry to the party room. As your guests arrive, they have to be "cleared."

One of the most exciting things about going to the Stork Club was knowing that you were sure to see celebrities! It was not unusual to see Cary Grant and Greer Garson sweeping past the gold chain after her final curtain call in Broadway's *Destry Rides Again*. Or to bump into Frank Sinatra on the dance floor of the Shermane Suite as Walter Winchell called in notes for his column. Few of us can include contemporary celebrities on our guest lists, but you can invite your guests to come as their favorite movie star or recording artist. Pick an era. If you are hosting a seventy-fifth birthday party for your father, set the party in the decade he was born and ask your guests to come as their favorite celebrity couple: the Duke and Duchess of Windsor, Humphrey Bogart and Lauren Bacall, Lucille Ball and Desi Arnaz, or Katharine Hepburn and Spencer Tracy, to name a few. Or make someone a celebrity for the night. Write a press release about the guest or guests of honor (college graduate, engaged couple, etc.). Depending on where you live and the scope of your party, the social editor of your local daily or weekly newspaper may find it worth covering!

Flashbulbs were always popping at the Stork Club. Have someone take pictures dressed like Beautiful Mary, with rhinestone barrettes in her hair and wearing a white blouse and short black skirt. For a vintage feel, use black-and-white film. Take pictures of each guest or couple. After developing the film, place a photograph of each guest in a white paper frame on which you have written "Stork Club" and the date. When they receive your gift, it will always remind them of you and the unforgettable party you threw.

SHERMAN'S RULE #3:

Relax!

My father used to tell his staff: "Once the party starts, don't get nervous about foul-ups. They'll happen. Stay calm and smile, unless someone drops dead!" Was he remembering the day my pet monkey got loose and ran through the dining room in the midst of lunch hour? Or was he still laughing about the night Tallulah Bankhead beckoned him over and said, "Sherman, darling, this is the best steak I've ever eaten in a restaurant. It tastes . . . well . . . charbroiled." My father never let on that it was in deed charbroiled: the kitchen had just caught fire and all the meat had burned up!

Remember: Expect the unexpected, but don't let your guests know when something goes wrong.

Now that you've learned my father's approach to creating a memorable experience at the Stork Club, let's pick the right room for your event.

CUB ROOM

Your special dinner party for eight to ten guests should take place at Table 50, the most exclusive table in the Stork Club's most exclusive room. Leather banquettes and molded wood paneling lent an air of intimacy. Illustrated portraits of the Beautiful Girls (the models, actresses, and socialites who graced the covers of *Cosmopolitan, Good Housekeeping*, and *Redbook*) hung on the walls. An evening in the Cub Room meant gaiety, glamour, and gossip!

Wedding Anniversary / Engagement Dinner / Birthday

An intimate celebration for 8–10 guests

Invitations:

- Announce that you have reserved Table 50, the most famous table at the Stork Club
- Design your invitation as a speakeasy membership card, or include a password
- Ask guests to come as a celebrity whom they might have run into at the Stork Club
- Enclose a press release on your guest(s) of honor

Props:

- Gold chain (hook together two or three gold-plated link belts)
- Blowup portrait of guest(s) of honor

- 72-inch round table
- White tablecloth (dark green border optional)
- Solid white napkins, folded to stand
- Black ceramic ashtray (authentic Stork Club or plain black)
- Black ceramic water pitcher (authentic Stork Club or plain black)
- Stork figurine
- Centerpiece of red roses
- Champagne stand

Menu:

All food recipes arc taken from the Stork Club chef's original notes. In many cases, there are no indications as to the size of the portions or cooking time, so you should do at least one run-through before your event.

All cocktail recipes are from *The Stork Club Bar Book*, by Lucius Beebe, Rinehart & Company, Inc., New York, 1946. The book is out of print, but your library may have a copy of it.

Cocktails:

Stork Club Cocktail
dash of lime juice
juice of half an orange
dash of triple sec
1½ oz. gin
dash of Angostura bitters

Shake well and strain in a chilled 4-oz. glass.

Honeymoon
1½ oz. applejack
1½ oz. Benedictine
juice of half a lemon
3 dashes of curacao

Shake and serve in a 3-oz. glass.

- Scotch and soda, with glass swizzle sticks
- Martinis
- Old-fashioneds

Wines and Champagnes:

Lucius Beebe observed that:

- Taste in table wines at the Stork Club ran almost exclusively to claret and Burgundy, as well as German wines of the Rhine.
- Ten bottles of champagne were served for every bottle of still wine. The favorites at the Stork Club were Bollinger, Veuve Clicquot, Mumm, and Dom Perignon.

Canapés:

- Pigs-in-a-blanket (miniature franks), with frilly toothpicks
- Pâté

Appetizer:

- Shrimp, lobster, or crabmeat cocktail
- *(Iced bawl of olives, radishes, scallions, and celery hearts, and a basket of French rolls on the table)*

Entrées:

CHICKEN À LA CHESTERFIELD

(A FAVORITE OF WALTER WINCHELL'S)

Alternate slices of roast turkey (Surprise! It wasn't made with chicken!) and baked ham on a broiler pan. Top with broccoli. Spoon sauce over meat and broccoli and broil.

Sauce (makes 2 cups):

- Melt 1½ tbs. butter or margarine in saucepan.
- Stir in 1½ tbs. flour.
- Heat and gradually add 1½ cups light cream combined with ½ cup milk. Stir over low heat until mixture thickens. Simmer 5 minutes.
- Stir some of mixture into 2 beaten egg yolks.
- Return egg mixture to saucepan and heat a few minutes longer.
- Stir in 1 tbs. hollandaise sauce (homemade or bottled), 1½ tbs. prepared mustard,¾ tsp. salt, dash of pepper, 2 tbs. heavy whipping cream.

ROAST OF VEAL WITH CUB SAUCE
(A FAVORITE OF SONJA HENIE'S)

5-to-6-lb. boned loin of veal
½ cup vegetable oil
5 tbs. unsalted butter
salt and pepper
diced celery and carrots
½ cup port wine
½ cup stock
1 bouquet garni (celery, thyme, bay leaf, parsley—tied in a bunch)

Preheat oven to 400 degrees. Heat oil and butter in a roasting pan over medium-high heat. Season veal with salt and pepper and brown lightly on all sides. Remove the veal and stir in the diced celery and carrots. Add ¼ cup port, ¼ cup stock, and the bouquet garni.

Return veal to pan and roast in oven, covered, for 35 minutes. Add remaining port and stock and continue cooking for an additional 20 minutes. Remove veal from oven and let stand for 10 minutes, covered in aluminum foil, while preparing sauce.

Serve with snow peas and wild rice.
Sauce (makes 1 cup):

- In a small saucepan, combine ¼ cup melted currant jelly, ¼ cup pan juices, ½ cup port wine.
- Bring to a boil and simmer 5 minutes.
- Add 2 tsp. ground ginger, 2 tsp. dry mustard, ⅛ tsp. salt.
- Cook a few minutes longer; stir in juice from 1 lemon.

Dessert:

PINEAPPLE À LA STORK
Quarter a pineapple lengthwise, including the leaves. Hull and slice fruit and return to shell. For each portion, serve one quarter of pineapple with a few sections of grapefruit and orange. Place a scoop of lemon sorbet in the center and top with a maraschino cherry. Sprinkle with Cointreau. (For a birthday party, place a candle in the sorbet.)

BLESSED EVENT ROOM
This large private room on the second floor of the Stork Club had its own bar and service kitchen. It accommodated approximately one hundred guests but could be partitioned for smaller gatherings. It was where I celebrated my preadolescent birthdays, when little girls wore velvet dresses with touches of lace, little boys

donned bow ties with short pants and knee socks, and patent leather was on every foot. There was plenty of room for musical chairs and Pin the Hat on the Stork. No one shushed us. My father loved children and he wanted the Stork Club to be a place where you could feel comfortable bringing the entire family.

Baby Shower / Child's Birthday / Milestone Birthday
A youthful occasion for 25–50 guests

Invitations:

- Buy boxed invitations with a stork motif
- Purchase diaper pins (kilt pins will work, too) and fasten to a handwritten memo providing details about the event

Props:

- White and gold helium balloons
- Poster board of a stork with separate cutout of top hat (used for Pin the Hat on the Stork)

Entertainment:

• Rent a VCR and select an age-appropriate movie for your guest of honor.

Children:
Little Miss Marker (Shirley Temple)
National Velvet (Elizabeth Taylor)
The Secret Garden (Margaret O'Brien)

All of these child stars grew up at the Stork Club
Adults:
The Stork Club (Betty Hutton and Barry Fitzgerald)
• Teach your children or grandchildren the Bunny Hop, Lindy, or Charleston!

Menu:

All food recipes are taken from the Stork Club chef's original notes. In many cases, there are no indications as to the size of the portions or cooking time, so you should do at least one run-through before your event.

All cocktail recipes are from *The Stork Club Bar Book*, by Lucius Beebe, Rinehart & Company, Inc., New York, 1946. The book is out of print, but your library may have a copy of it.

Cocktails:

BLESSED EVENT
　juice of half a lime dash
　dash of curaçao
　2 oz. Benedictine
　2 oz. applejack

Shake and strain. Serve in a cocktail glass.

CHAMPAGNE COCKTAIL
　chilled champagne
　1 lump of sugar, saturated with Angostura bitters
　1 cube of ice
　twist of lemon peel
　Serve in champagne glass.

SHIRLEY TEMPLE (NONALCOHOLIC)
  ginger ale
  maraschino cherry

Serve in a champagne glass.

Canapés:

- Children:
  Pretzels
  Popcorn
  Cubes of cheese
- Adults:

  Cheese platter
  Smoked salmon and cucumber on pumpernickel triangles
  (Iced bawl of olives, radishes, scallions, and celery hearts, and a basket of French rolls on every table)

Entrées:

CHICKEN BURGER À LA STORK

(A FAVORITE OF IRVING BERLIN'S)

- Finely grind the meat from a 5-lb. chicken.
- Mix in a dash each of salt, pepper, and nutmeg.
- Add 1 oz. soft butter.
- Add ½ pint heavy cream.
- Mix well.
- Shape into patties.
- Dip each patty quickly in melted butter, sprinkle with fresh bread crumbs, and broil about 10 minutes, turning and coloring both sides.

Serve with a hot tomato sauce, French-fried sweet potatoes, and fresh peas.

BILLINGSLEY CHOP SUEY
(CREATED ESPECIALLY FOR MARGARET O'BRIEN)

- Melt 1 tbs. butter or margarine in a Dutch oven.
- Stir in 1 cup washed, drained wild rice; heat for 5 minutes.
- Add

3 beef bouillon cubes dissolved in 3 cups boiling water
1 cup sliced celery hearts
1 cup coarsely chopped lettuce
1 cup coarsely chopped raw spinach
¾ tsp.salt
speck of pepper

- Simmer, covered, for 20 minutes, then turn heat very low and cook about 30 minutes, or until liquid has been absorbed.
- Meanwhile, pan-broil until medium done two 10-oz. bone less rib steaks.
- Cut into 1-inch pieces; toss with rice mixture. Serve hot.

Makes 4 servings

Dessert:

STORK SNOWBALLS

- Individual scoops of vanilla ice cream covered with
  coconut flakes
  chocolate sauce
  colored sprinkles

For a child's party, put a candle in each scoop of ice cream and present them all on a platter as you would a cake. Let the birthday celebrant blow out all the candles and then present individual servings.

For a baby shower, alternate pink and blue candles in each scoop of ice cream. Let all of the guests blow out their candles to celebrate the impending arrival.

SHERMAINE SUITE

The consummate party space, the Shermane Suite was the largest room in the Stork Club. Square in shape, it was swathed in aquamarine drapery. Gold braid festooned the fabric to frame arched mirror panels. Here, the music never stopped, with two bands alternating until closing time at 3 p.m. Couples crushed onto the dance floor, ice cubes clinked, and flames from Cherries Jubilee, Crêpes Suzette, and Baked Alaska competed with Elizabeth Taylor's diamonds.

My father liked up-tempo and never allowed a slow waltz, except for the Duke and Duchess of Windsor. Choose either the big band sound or Broadway show tunes from the forties and fifties. End your party with a conga line as your guests pick up their coats.

Balloon Night and New Year's Eve

A romantic night of dining and dancing for 50 or more guests

Invitations:

- Shiny white invitations printed in gold, or shiny black invitations printed in white, each with burgundy or dark green tassels
- Balloons printed with party information

Props:

- Gold chain (hook together two or three gold-plated link belts)
- Party hats and horns
- Red bow ties for gents
- White cotton gloves for ladies
- Netting for ceiling (use fish or tennis netting)
- Balloons in assorted colors

Entertainment:

Make this a Balloon Night! At the Stork Club, my father would hang a fishnet over the dance floor filled with hundreds of gaily colored balloons. Some balloons contained crisp hundred-dollar bills; some round-trip tickets to Hollywood; others held slips of pa per to be redeemed for a Cadillac, a thousand-dollar bottle of per fume, or a pedigreed puppy. The balloons were released at midnight, and captains hurried around the dance floor with hat pins while the most sophisticated people in the world waited with childlike anticipation.

Your prizes need not be expensive or outrageous. Go for whimsy: a gift certificate for a shoe shine, a hansom ride through the park, a small telescope to watch "the stars." It's not about the cost, but rather caring about how much your friends enjoy the evening.

Menu:

All food recipes arc taken from the Stork Club chef's original notes. In many cases, there are no indications as to the size of the portions or cooking time, so you should do at least one run-through before your event.

All cocktail recipes are from *The Stork Club Bar Book*, by Lucius Beebe, Rinehart & Company, Inc .. New York, 1946. The book is out of print, but your library may have a copy of it.

Cocktails:

DRY MARTINI
  ½ oz. London or dry gin
  ½ oz. French vermouth

Stir, decorate with an olive, and sen1e in a 3-oz. cocktail glass.

ORCHID COCKTAIL
  dash of Crême Yvette
  white of one egg
  2 oz. gin

Shake hard and strain. Serve in a chilled 4-oz. wineglass. (Use only a dash of Crême Yvette. It will produce a delightful violet flavor, with a color as nice as an orchid flower.)

ROMANCE COCKTAIL
  ½ oz.brandy (cognac) and curaçao mixed in equal parts
  ½ oz. Amer Picon
  ½ oz. French vermouth
  ½ oz. Italian vermouth

Add cracked ice and shake. Serve in a cocktail glass.

CHAMPAGNE PUNCH (MAKES 1 GALLON)
  2 qt. champagne
  1 pony maraschino
  3 ponies brandy
  1 pony curaçao
  dash yellow chartreuse
  juice of 4 lemons
  2 qt. sparkling water
  sugar to taste
  fresh berries

Place a block of ice (or lots of ice cubes) in punch bowl, pour punch over, and serve.

Wines and Champagnes:

Lucius Beebe obseived that:

- Taste in table wines at the Stork Club ran almost exclu sively to claret and Burgundy, as well as German wines of the Rhine.

• Ten bottles of champagne were served for every bottle of still wine. The favorites at the Stork Club were Bollinger, Veuve Clicquot, Mumm, and Dom Pérignon.

Canapés:

• Quail eggs topped with caviar
• Thinly sliced beef rolled around scallions
• Asparagus tips rolled in smoked ham

Appetizer:

• Endive salad with blue cheese, walnuts, and sliced orange

Serve with:

CHUTNEY DRESSING
    ¼ cup chopped chutney
    ½ cup salad oil
    2 tbs. vinegar
    1 tsp. salt
    ½ tsp. pepper
    1 clove garlic

Mix ingredients together and mariante 1 to 2 hours. Remove clove of garlic. Shake and serve with endive salad.

(Iced bowl of olives, radishes, scallions, and celery hearts, and a basket of French rolls on every table)
    Entrées

STEAK DIANE

(A FAVORITE OF DOROTHY LAMOUR'S)
    thinly pounded slices of steak
    lightly toasted slices of white bread
    thinly sliced onion
    thinly sliced tomato
    pickle relish

The secret to the success of Steak Diane is to keep everything thinly sliced and flattened!

Quickly sauté meat and place on top of bread. Top with onion, tomato, and relish. Cut in quarters and serve with Spooner Steak Sauce.

Spooner Steak Sauce

- Sauté ½ cup finely chopped onions in ⅛ lb. butter until onions are golden.
- Add 1 bottle A.1 steak sauce.
- Add 1 pint heavy cream.
- Add 1 tsp. English mustard.
- Stir.
- Add ¼ cup chopped chives.
- Add 1 tsp. oregano.
- Bring ingredients to a boil and then simmer 5 minutes.
- Add juice of 1 lemon and a few drops Tabasco.

BEEF BOURGEOISIE
(A FAVORITE OF JOHN WAYNE'S)

4-lb. rump of beef
diced onions and carrots
1 cup flour
3 quarts boiling stock or water
1 pint red wine
3 cups canned stewed tomatoes
2 crushed cloves of garlic
1 bouquet garni (celery, thyme, bay leaf, parsley—tied in a bunch salt and
   pepper)
1 glass Madeira wine

In a saute pan with a little fat, brown the beef. When brown, remove the meat from the pan.

Using the same pan, fry diced onions and carrots until slightly brown. Add flour and fry just a little. Add boiling stock of water, red wine, and stewed tomatoes. Stir well and let boil a few minutes. Add garlic, bouquet garni, salt, and pepper.

Place the beef in the sauce and cook on low heat for 3 hours or so, depending upon the tenderness of the meat. When done, remove the beef and strain the sauce. Remove all the grease that appears on top of the sauce. Test for seasoning. Pour in Madeira wine. Put meat back in the sauce and let it boil a few minutes.

Slice the meat against the grain and serve with garnish of cooked car rots, small braised white onions, new peas, and Madeira sauce.

Madeira Sauce

Reduce 1 glass of Madeira wine with a little sugar. Add pan juices and let boil a few minutes.

Desserts:

CRÊPES SUZETTE À LA STORK

The crêpes are prepared in advance; the rest is showmanship!
  6 sugar lumps
  1 orange
  1 lemon
  ⅓ cup orange juice
  ½ cup butter or margarine
  2 tbs. granulated sugar
  ¼ cup Cointreau or curaçao
  2 tbs. rum or Benedictine
  ⅓ cup brandy or Grand Marnier

Rub lump sugar on rinds of orange and lemon; add lumps to orange juice; crush until dissolved.

Melt butter or margarine in chafing dish and add orange juice mix ture and granulated sugar; heat. Place crêpes, folded in quarters, in sauce; ladle sauce over crêpes until they are saturated. Mix Coin treau or curaçao and rum or Benedictine and pour over crêpes. Pour on brandy or Grand Marnier but do not stir.

When mixture is heated, tilt pan to flame so sauce catches fire. Spoon flaming sauce over crêpes. Serve crêpes and sauce on heated plates.

SORBET

If you are intimidated by fireworks, there is nothing more classic and elegant than an assortment of sorbets garnished with mint leaves and raspberries. Serve with petit fours.

So there you have it. If you follow the three basic principles that my father practiced—prepare, make your guests feel special, and relax—and select a room that is appropriate to the occasion, you are ready to host your own Stork Club party!

Writing this has given me an opportunity to relive some priceless childhood memories. In fact, I can't wait to host my next Stork Club party! Now whose birthday is coming up ... ?

CHEERFULLY,

SHERMANE

New York City
October 2001

Index